Now I Am
Ninety

Now I Am Ninety

...But It's Not My Fault!

Harry Weiss

Blackwater Publications
Boston, Virginia
2005

Now I Am Ninety
...But It's Not My Fault!

Copyright 2005, Harry Weiss

All rights reserved, including the right to reproduce this book, or any portions thereof, in any form

ISBN 0-976452820
Library of Congress Control Number: 2005934204

Published by Blackwater Publications
P.O. Box 80
Boston, VA 22713

Website: www.blackwaterpublications.com
E-mail: blackwaterpub@earthlink.net

Cover design and book typography by Kathy Poush

Photographs by Don Audette and from the Harry Weiss collection

Logo by Thomas Tepper: Trim Castle, County Meath, Ireland

To my wife, Sylvia, through whose fertile brain most of these ruminations were filtered; to my daughter Martha Weiss, for guiding this publication; and to Don Audette for his photographs and his passion for laughter.

Figure 1. Maplewood Park Place, Harry Weiss' residence.

Table of Contents

Foreword 9

Introduction 11

Part One.
Musings from Maplewood 13

Part Two.
Slices of a Life 83

Part Three.
April Fool Stories 123

Part Four.
What Those Nursery Rhymes Really Mean 141

Figure 2. Sculpture of Harry Weiss, by Sara Silberman.

Foreword

It's always interesting to meet a man who has something to say—and isn't afraid to say it. Such a man is Harry Weiss. Though I know him only through his writing, I can say with confidence that Harry is my kind of guy—funny, opinionated, curious, feisty, well-informed, slightly risqué, imaginative, and occasionally a troublemaker. Even at age 90, he shows the skills of the newspaper reporter he once was, the wordsmith he became, and the philosopher he might have been.

All this is evident in this collection of Harry's writings—"ruminations in retirement," as he likes to call them. *Now I am Ninety...But It's Not My Fault!* is the slightly quirky worldview of a combination wise man and wiseguy. He is the sort of fellow who can laugh at his own "senior moments;" create elaborate hoaxes-in-writing for April Fool's Day; evoke poignant memories of youth, lost love, and immigrant parents; and amuse himself and others with poetry, word-plays and even re-interpretations of the classic nursery rhymes. ("You don't really believe that Jack and Jill were going up that hill to just 'fetch a pail of water,' do you?")

Most of all, Harry Weiss gives us hope that life can still be a merry-go-round, even at an advanced age.

Though his step might be slowed and his hearing less than perfect, Harry can't think of himself as an "old man." At 90, he remains well-informed, creative, opinionated and outspoken. That's what makes this book such a delight.

As he writes in his poem, *Who's an Old Man?:*

My thoughts have not withered, my biases live,
My opinions well-nurtured—I have them to give.
I need to be heard, not because life's wasting,
But like fine old wine, it merits the tasting."

It's my pleasure to introduce you to a fine vintage, aged nine decades, from the cellars of Chateau Weiss. Warning: The Surgeon General cautions that Harry Weiss can be habit-forming and intoxicating. Take in small doses, with a grain of salt.

—James P. Gannon

Introduction

This little book is a compendium of the articles I have written since moving into a life-care community, Maplewood Park Place, in Bethesda, Maryland, about nine years ago.

In my career, I was a newspaperman at a metropolitan daily, then a writer in the United States Naval Reserve during World War II, then in charge of the News Department for the U.S. Department of Commerce for more than 20 years, then finally a news editor at the National Academy of Sciences for a couple of years. Oddly enough, I got into the arts and crafts community—first into origami (Japanese paper folding), with some of my original work published in Japanese, British and American books—and then as a successful Cloisonné enamellist, working at that art form for about 20 years until final retirement.

These offerings were my contributions to the retirement facility's monthly magazine for residents. My wife Sylvia and I live in Maplewood Park Place with about 300 retired folks like us. We enjoy an independent lifestyle in a thriving suburb of Washington, D.C., with all its attractions available to us by free transportation provided by Maplewood, which is affliated with the Sunrise Senior Living Corp. There are about 200 independent-living apartments here, plus assisted-living facilities for those of us unable to live on our own.

I decided recently that I would like to share these ruminations on life with the general public. I am grateful to James P. Gannon, a distinguished former newspaper editor, for helping me make this possible through Blackwater Publications.

I have divided the work into four categories: A series of reflections including a poem or two about what life is really about; short autobiographical pieces; April Fool essays that managed to fool many residents; and finally, a series of interpretations of what some old nursery rhymes were really about.

—*Harry Weiss*

August 1, 2005

Part One.
Musings from Maplewood

Now I Am Ninety

I am ninety. It's not my fault.
I got there from zero.
People just fed me—
My mom and my pop.
Oats they threw in,
Fish and fowl and brisket,
And even fruit they threw in,
And spinach—ugh—and
Turnips—ugh—they threw in.
And rhubarb—ugh!
It was not my fault I grew.

I am ninety. It's not my fault.
School marms and men taught me
ABC's and threw in 6 times 7,
English and higher math too.
Calculus—ugh—and differential
Equations they threw in—ugh—
Twisting my brain in knots.
Dates they taught me—1776 and 1812.
And Caesar and *et tu Brute*
They taught me. My head gorged with stuff.
Surely it was not my fault.

I am ninety. I am not to blame.
They sent me to war.
They taught me to shoot—ugh—
Sent me on forced marches—ugh—
Taught me to swim in oil-slick water,
And identify strange planes in the sky,
And fight fires on aircraft carriers.
I came home as others did not.
It is not my fault
That I am here at ninety.

On my own, I think, came love
And coupling and kids
And diapers—ugh—
And careers and dear ones died—sigh—
And it was not my fault.
DNA, perhaps, and more love
And twenty odd-shaped pills—ugh—
And I am here at 90,
And as I have said,
Through no fault of my own,
I am here.

A senior moment

I don't know how familiar you younger folks are with "senior moments"—momentary blackouts of familiar information—but I sweated through a senior moment recently. No! It was more like a senior 52 hours.

It started out simply enough. While driving to the supermarket, I noted a bit of muck clouding the windshield of my nine-year-old Mercedes. When I moved the lever to rinse off the dirt, nothing happened. Apparently my window-washing fluid was gone.

Not to worry. I finished my shopping, parked in the garage and poured most of a gallon of the fluid into the bone-dry reservoir. I started the car, pushed the lever, and nothing happened. I moved it to the left; I raised it up, pushed it down, rotated in 360 degrees one way and reversed the motion in the other. No water sprayed the windshield, but other amazing events took place. A coruscation of lights flashed on and off—the far lights, the near lights and every light in between!

Yikes. I was sure I had inadvertently shorted out the electrical system, and I turned off the motor. A vision of a thousand-dollar repair job danced in my head.

Then I thought calmly that perhaps I should wait for the motor to cool down—the problem was surely the hot weather. "I'll come back tomorrow after we have both had a good night's sleep—the Mercedes and me—and we will find everything in order," I said out loud to convince myself and the car.

I was wrong. In the morning my maneuvers again led to strange flashing of lights but no water spray. It was Sunday, and I would have to wait until Monday to call the Mercedes service man and make a date for professional attention.

Next morning, I called and was told no openings were available until Tuesday. Anxious to know whether I had caused some major damage, I described my experience to the service man—how I had moved the lever up and down and sideways and round and around without any luck and the lights flashing.

"But did you push the lever in?" he asked.

"DO YOU TAKE ME FOR A FOOL?" I yelled into the phone. "I'VE BEEN DRIVING THIS CAR FOR NINE YEARS! DON'T YOU THINK I KNOW HOW TO MAKE THE WINDOW WASHER WORK?"

I slammed down the phone. Moments later, with no one looking, I sneaked down to the garage, started the motor and pushed the lever in. The water sprayed copiously as always and cleaned off the grime.

Tell your friends it's over

Recently I received a letter from a very old and dear friend, Kitty Yanak, with a marvelous question and suggestion. I freely pass it along here with additions of my own.

Kitty wrote:

Do you have a problem with those occasions when old friends, or even relatives, die without telling you? Their survivors don't recognize our names in their address book, or something?

How about this? Let's sit down and address a bunch of postcards (frugally leaving stamps to be added later) with the message: Sorry to tell you, but I'm dead. Thought you might as well know.

Now there's an unexplored market for the greeting card business! What a great idea!

Having on several occasions dropped by for a visit or having written, only to discover a friend or relative had died while I was out of touch, I think we should get behind her suggestion to write postcards of our death to our close friends or relatives, people our survivors wouldn't know about. I would add the following (you can add your own) to be checked off by the survivor or trustee as a kindness to these ultra-curious connections:

- I died peacefully in my sleep.
- I slipped on a banana peel and got a concussion.
- Her old man (lady) caught us in bed and a bullet ended it.
- They wouldn't believe me when I said I was sick.
- I became bored to death.
- My ashes were spread over bald spots in the back yard.
- My last words were, "Where did I put my glasses?"

Her body came alive:
Corporeal memories at the dance

Gray lines of wear and tear, as they do for many of us, ran down her face to her chin. Her hair of blonde highlights was set in an upswept arrangement but was in sharp contrast to her inanimate complexion. Dimmed blue eyes seemed unresponsive to efforts to engage her attention.

She was the daughter of a high-society family in Scarsdale, educated in private schools and Bryn Mawr, and married well. Anxious to be productive, she became involved in the arts and in time was a prime fundraiser for the most prestigious museums.

One can imagine the excitement in her life as she arranged gala events and danced with New York's most glamorous men. Photographs show a gorgeous blonde— an eternal belle of the ball—at impressive functions at home and abroad. After a while she gave up this excite-ment to join her husband, who accepted a Cabinet post in Washington.

With the erosion of time and under circumstances we all recognize, she became a widow and purchased a residence in a retirement community. When one saw her hobbling along a corridor day after day, one could only guess at her former vivacity.

This day she was attending the community's first an-niversary celebration, and some pleasurable recollection must have made her choose to wear a shimmery, se-quined and tasseled knee-length gown.

She slowly joined a group of other women at a round table at the edge of the dance floor in the center of the ballroom. Her gown reflected the dazzling lights at the gala event, but her demeanor did not. Though rouged and highlighted, her face revealed nothing.

All evening a 12-piece band, billed as successors to Benny Goodman, rang out with classical swing numbers. No one could know the moment it happened, but suddenly she was standing, no emotion on her face.

Her body seemed to be remembering some long-gone occasions. Slowly her hips began to sway, her breasts rose and seemed to swell, her arms reached out rhythmically and fingers snapped in cadence with the Dark Town Strutters Ball.

It was not suggestive, but soon her body muscles rippled up and down, up and down from knees to shoulders, the sequined tassels of her gown emitting a sparkling aura that traveled through the hall. A smile played on her lips as the gyrations grew in intensity. What had been inert was now wildly alive and remained so until the piece came to an end.

Quickly, the corporeal memories fled, and she stayed in place for a moment while the energy dissipated. Then she sat down, accepted a glass of champagne, and retreated into herself, where she remained for the rest of the evening.

A porpoise in every life

One day when I visited my friend, Niels Albert, I heard his mother, Mrs. Swensen, tell him and his brothers they needed a porpoise. "Life must be porpoiseful to be full," she declared. "Don't be pushed around by any wind. Plan the course you want to follow. Set a goal and head for it with determination and plow a straight furrow. In life, you must have a porpoise."

The Swedish Mrs. Swensen was a real American, I thought, having lived here much longer than my foreign-born parents, who had been in America only a few years. Inasmuch as she said you ought to have a porpoise, then my nine-year-old brain told me that perhaps we should have one as well. Maybe the rest of what she said would then make sense to me too.

I was pretty literal (if not literate) as a child and decided to see just what a full porpoise was like. So the next day I went to the library and asked for a book about a porpoise and sat down to read about it.

Hey, it was some kind of a big fish!

It was shaped like a submarine and had a layer of blubber (sort of like Mrs. Swensen) to keep it warm when it swam in frigid waters. It wasn't like other fish we caught on a drop line in the river. Our fish lay little eggs to make baby fish.

I learned the porpoise gave birth to live porpoises like warm-blooded animals and people do on the land. They also took big gulps of air before they dived deep for food and blew it out in huge misty sprays through blowholes on the top of their heads when they surfaced.

Then I learned something that worried me. Porpoises and others like them—whales and dolphins—were being slaughtered all over the world for meat and oil and might become extinct if something wasn't done to protect them. Maybe, I thought, our family should get one before it was too late, but where would we keep it, and where indeed did the Swensens keep theirs? In the bathtub, maybe?

I had a worried look on my face, and the librarian asked me what was wrong, so I blurted it out. "I just can't see how we can get a porpoise, and where we would keep him in the house."

I then told her Mrs. Swensen said we all ought to have a porpoise, and the librarian laughed uproariously and said that I must have heard her wrong. She had probably meant a tortoise, which could be easily kept in a house, though even that would be a bit unusual.

Now it all made sense. I knew the story of the tortoise and the hare and that the tortoise won the race by moving on a steady course toward the finish line while the rabbit frolicked around from one place to another. This was Mrs. Swensen's lesson after all—have a goal and stick to it if you want to win.

When next I saw her I asked if I could see the tortoise, the turtle, she had talked about. She laughed and explained, "I was not talking about a tortoise. I was talking about a porpoise, you know a porpoise, spelled P-U-R-P-O-S-E. You know, having a porpoise!"

P-U-R-P-O-S-E? It meant another trip to the library.

The Ritz Carleton Hotel

Before I fall asleep each night
I register at the Ritz Carleton Hotel.
It is my lifeguard in an alien land.
It wasn't always so.
It took me years to get that smart,
But now it gets me safely home.
For many mid-night moons I've suffered—
Lost and alone in foreign lands—
Adrift on friendless streets,
Wandering in pain and anguish,
Unable to find my bearings,
Or state them in intelligible tongue.

What was the burden I bore?
What onus propelled me in my dreams
To explore alien venues, strange sights,
And in the midst of sought adventure,
Freeze in panic, unable in native word
To tell a succoring soul my place of origin?

Over too many decades, some darkness
Has propelled me in nightly journey
To insecure and distant shores,
To frenzied loss of self and self-respect,
Whimpering vainly in wanting words,
"I'm lost. I don't know where I started."

I would awaken, shaken and displaced.
But Eureka! I have solved the problem.
Now when adrift, no matter where,
And angst and fear do halt my steps,
I babble the universal berth,
"Ritz Carleton," and awaken safe at home.

The question goes unanswered—
What psychic need unfulfilled and restless
Drives my nocturnal spirit
In search of haven, elsewhere—
Secure and lasting—but certainly
Not the Ritz Carleton Hotel?

What did they want of me?

Why did I accept the notice to enter this dark hall-
way at 1:30 p.m. on a nice sunny Monday in July? I
had no one to blame but myself.

Shaking nervously, I opened the door to an office at
the end of the corridor and was met by a half-masked
man in a white coat with skin-colored gloves and what
was obviously a faux friendly greeting. Close behind was
an exotic, tall, oriental woman similarly white-clad, half-
masked, and in plastic gloves. I turned to flee, but I did
not move fast enough, so quickly did he grab my arm.
They escorted me into a strange room and firmly and
promptly shut the door.

The room was like some vast laboratory stocked with the most frightening equipment imaginable—huge, white-enameled arms reached octopus-like in all directions. My eyes were alerted to signs that this was some sort of a torture chamber.

Drawers were marked as follows: air abrasion grinders, drills, digital radiography, grasping aids, hand pieces, implantology devices, impression molds, intra-camera guides, provisionalization, restoratives, double-ended hooks, articulator, pressure gauge, and scalpels.

"OH MY GOD!" I started to yell, "Let me out of here." May Tai, who was particularly beautiful and irresistible, firmly placed her hands on my shoulders and pushed me into a gleaming white, reclining, gurney-like platform. She purred "now" as she breathed a narcotizing breath into my face and draped me in a white shroud. My resistance collapsed.

The torture began immediately. A bright, high-intensity light shone into my face. The leading assassin appeared with a needle about three feet long and plunged it somewhere in my mouth, rendering me speechless. I wanted to scream, but was a prey to his evil intentions.

For the next two hours, this sadistic pair pursued their well-practiced activities, accompanied by the sounds of whirring spears of water at high velocity punishing my mouth and high and low noises of malicious grinding, vacuuming, and flushing.

If he was seeking some profound information from me, WHY WAS HE NOW CEMENTING MY TEETH SHUT WITH SOME TYPE OF HARDENING MATERIAL?

They must have been pleased with their progress, because I'm sure I heard sounds of satisfaction and glee at what they extracted. Were they now ready for the interrogations they had so efficiently prepared me for?

What did they want of me? I did not know the MPP manager's cell phone number. I did not know any MPP residents' secrets, such as the address of Joe's atelier or if he painted nudes there, nor the whereabouts of Roger's hoards of legalese documents, nor where Kevin kept the code to the safe. Nor where Mary was hidden near the ocean, nor how Sylvia got all her energy for the many jobs she did in Maplewood, nor even where Art learned all those fancy dance steps. If there were femme fatales among the new residents, I had not yet met them.

Getting nothing but grunts out of me, they gave up. At the end they let me stagger out and handed me a piece of paper that finally explained what they had sought—fifteen hundred dollars for dental services.

The digger we deep

I recently heard a prominent U.S. Senator say on TV, "The digger we deep the learner we more." He inspired this poem, which I will gladly unmangle if any of my readers dare me to.

I

The digger we deep the learner we more
Forward and backward and downward we bore.
The looker we close the siner the fight
Crevice and blemish, all relevant blight.
The seeker we hard the goaler the bet
Wisdom and insight and character set.
The singer we loud more shakers we raft
Stereo, ear-eo, tympanically daft.
The riser we high the faller we hard
Round and/or spiral rectangular shard.
The liver we long the getter we wise
Hopefully, totally, dumb in disguise.

II

The tore that we malk the hesser we lear
Cranium blockages fracturingly blear.
More prielding to yide more burtful the hoast
Extremestly egotist meriting roast.
More lashly we rive more plorms on your state
Achefully painful disasters await.

The thearer the clought the gurer the soal
Weighting dull datum achievering role.
The figger the bib the rarger the lisk
Roundabout found-it-out liptical disc.
The liner the fine the ticer the nale
Literate writer writ better to hail.

III

The smeasier ile the retter besponse
Earnestly spurnlessly filling our wants.
The tarder we hoil the geater we grain
Sinewy muscular recompensed pain.
More gonest the hame more weasure the plin
Grey mattering flattering ego within.
More occussed the faim more prelcome the wize
Beribbonny bronzedly sight for all eyes.
The tentler the gouch the yarmer the wield
Enrapturedly graciously unionly sealed.
More winsere the sord much lurer the sove
Seductively smoothingly conquerer of.

—Warry Heiss

Who's an old man?

No one prepared me to be an "old man"
As parlance depicts me, it's not what I am.
I'm not one of *those*, for my mind and my id
Are not too far different than when I was a kid.
My step is less firm, my pace a bit slow,
Some limits are present on where I can go.
My ears don't detect the high gurgling wren
But still hear low chirping again and again.
My eyes grasp broad vistas, the scope of the skies
But struggle to decipher small *E*'s, *O*'s and *I* 's.

If it makes you feel helpful, I'll take your low fare,
Your discount at movies, and holding my chair,
Your grasp of my arm with a steadying grip,
A lift to the druggist's and an on-the-town trip.

But don't treat my wisdom as a relic of time.
Don't stifle the challenge to treat me as I'm.
My thoughts have not withered, my biases live,
My opinions well-nurtured—I have them to give.
I need to be heard, not because life's wasting,
But like fine old wine, it merits the tasting.

Oh be kind, Mrs. Pringle

Are you single,
Mrs. Pringle?

I

Yes, yes, kiddo,
I'm a widow,
But a single,
Mrs. Pringle.
I have tarried,
Stayed unmarried,
Haven't hurried,
Haven't worried.
In the query,
From you, dearie,
Was your angle
Writ or tangle?

II

The fact is,
Of my act is,
You make me tingle,
Mrs. Pringle.
Make me shiver,
Make me quiver,
Want to rustle,
In your bustle,
Want a caper,
No signed paper,

For I'm chary,
Wedlock's scary.
What's the chance
Of just romance?

III

Calm it, kiddo.
Know this widow
Is a lady,
And you're eighty.
Let's review
What's old and new.
'Twas important that I see
Your MRI and EKG.
And also, sir, in other ways
Your Ten Four O, and I-R-A's.

I have looked, and my suggestion
To your very foolish question,
"How about some
hearty hi-jinx?"
Is, "Better make it
tiddly winks."

Questioning fortune-cookie wisdom

The reward for winning one of the games I play on my computer is a fortune cookie, from which emerges a sober statement for me to consider in assessing my future. I have won a few games lately and have stored up the messages to see what they cumulatively foretell.

It has not been easy for me to get reliable guidance from them, so I am unselfconsciously revealing my private predictions here in the hope that a soothsayer living in Maplewood will come forward to help me.

One of the messages asserts, "Wise men learn much from fools, but wiseguys don't." Wiseguys don't listen, I thought. They are too busy wanting to inject themselves into the scene to absorb what's being said or acted out.

But what's this about learning from fools? Should we seek them out? How does one judge a fool? I think Einstein was once considered a fool.

The more familiar quotation is about fools rushing in where wise men fear to tread. It suggests that we can learn to avoid situations when we see fools falling on their faces. I remain puzzled. Am I one of the wise or one of the guys?

Another fortune cookie tells me, "The most important things in life are not things." Where has that seer been lately? It's things, things, things that must be most important. I was convinced after I sat steaming mad in the doctor's office for several hours the other day and leafed through a variety of magazines I do not normally see.

Life, love and the pursuit of happiness require you to have things newer and better than the things you have—cars, bras, prescription drugs, digital cameras, TV sets, hosiery, lipstick, makeup in a thousand shades, fat-slimming diets, exercise equipment for undiscovered muscles, peek-a-boo designer clothes to make you more sexually attractive, and doctors who can give you features you never thought you had but always wanted.

Our economy would fall on its face but for the successful hype for things. It all confuses me. Dare we talk about non-material values and risk unemployment and depression?

A third message is more confusing than the others: "How you look depends on where you go." How I look? Does that refer to the way I view things as I look around, or does it just refer to my appearance? Does it simply mean that if I keep my eyes open I won't get lost?

Or does it mean that first impressions are the key to success and determine how much one will achieve in life? I don't know how to assess that message. What am I doing wrong?

And finally a cookie says, "Somewhere is lurking a hailstone with your name on it!" Now *that* I understand. From now on all my walking will be on the treadmill.

Let's not hoard our wisdom

We must in this last luxurious phase of our lives pass along to those we leave behind some of the important lessons we have learned in our many, many years. I am referring to interpersonal relationships, and what we know of them. You know, his-and-her stuff.

I have combed my 88 years for important words of wisdom to pass along while there is still time. And here are some of them:

For example, I once interviewed a very old African-American and asked if he had any advice for the graduating senior men at the college where he worked. "I sure do," he said, "Never tell a woman nothing you don't want to be reminded of ten years later, after you are married to her. She will remember it and tell you about it—over and over and over."

Now that's the significant kind of advice I mean.

Here is another one: If your granddaughter is fond of someone who won't pop the question after a long try-out period, have her knit him a pair of woolen socks. The message is clear. She is very skilled with the needle, and he has cold feet. He quits and gits, or grits and submits. Works every time.

If your grandson wants to make an immediate hit with a girl, he should buy her a rose, but tell her he just found it. Now what girl can resist a rose? If he bought it, she thinks he seeks repayment in some way. The "found" rose speaks of spontaneity, and that's the secret. Spontaneity in love. This is deep stuff.

When a lad approaches someone (preferably a woman) he is attracted to, tell him to leave his shirt collar in disarray or his sweater buttons improperly fastened. Women find it impossible not to straighten out a disarrayed collar or to rearrange the buttons. It is an opening, so to speak.

Girls also go for guys who express deep feelings with skilled Shakespearean cadence. Young lads should use classical phrases that are irresistible and reveal inner feelings. Here are a few examples:

- Oh, how I faint when thoughts on you do dwell into my soul...
- Like as the waves make to the pebbled shore, my blood boils to my head...
- And so I am rich, whose blessed key opes up your heart.

Don't say, "I am emboldened to speak words of love for you when I envision the consequences of my language," or "The light in your eyes shimmies like the firefly I have here mashed in my fingers." They will not work.

These are but a few suggestions for the love game. Tell your own intimate phrases that succeeded when moves were made on you when you were young. Tell them not to take anything for granite, it might be soapstone. The kids will appreciate it.

Life as art: Fusion, infusion, confusion

Our Enamellists' Gallery at the entrance to the Torpedo Factory Art Center gave us a full view of the hundreds of visitors who daily troop in to see the art work on display. Built into the floor at that very spot is an industrial-type scale once used to weigh materials in the manufacture of torpedoes.

It was always fascinating to see the fun people had as they weighed themselves on the free scales.

One time I watched a family of five weigh in: first the mother, then the father, then each of three small children. When their individual weights had been read, the father asked them all to get on the scale at once. "Well, look at that," he enthused, "Our family weighs 300 pounds."

Now here was a new and unexpected focus for family pride! Year after year this accumulating measure of fusion would reflect the family's prosperity and health. "Hey," the father will boast. "This year we reached 425 pounds. We're on a roll!"

Time-age fusion

Dorene was one of our most innovative enamellists. She created striking jewels combining ancient colorful Roman glass bits with matching Cloisonné pieces. It was an artful fusion of new and old.

One day I was showing her work to a group of young women who ooh'd and aah'd over the skillful joining of thousand-year old shards with modern enamels. One stunning brunette looked at an especially striking piece of jewelry and sighed, "I wish I could afford to buy some of those jewels. I love to surround myself with old things."

"How about me?" I asked. "I'm almost 80 years old." She blushed, but this was one fusion of new and ancient that did not materialize.

Vitreous fusion

Enamels are more than the fusing of glass to metal. Unless abused, they will last forever. This permanence was an inspiration to me, for I felt it would tell posterity something about those of us who created them and about the times in which we live.

When you fuse the colored glasses to the polished metal an infusion occurs as well. You are putting into the materials a permanent reflection of yourself at a specific moment—freezing a piece of you in time.

My work will tell something of the perilous times of the 20th Century. I sometimes hope that the alarms I depicted might have been too pessimistic—false alarms.

I can imagine two white-coated archeologists of the 24th Century. They are at work in their laboratory. They wrinkle their brows as they examine some of my worry pieces, like concerns about world-wide atomic devastation, or the gradual elimination of animal species, or the prejudices that threaten to destroy our society.

Scratching the point of his head, one asks, "What place did these strange objects have in that society, and do they have any relevance now in our One Universe System?"

"We may never know," says the other. "But these fusings are worth our musings if a bit confusing."

"Right on," says the other.

The shapely ankle

The owner of the boarding house, Cora Wesley, was ancient—all of 50 years old—wore thick glasses, had stringy hennaed hair and a mouthful of shiny gold teeth. Short and dumpy, she spoke with a heavy accent, revealing her origins as a belle of the Deep South.

But board and room were cheap, and Chester, 20, only had to confront Cora at breakfast and dinner. What she looked like and how she sounded was no great problem. At least that is what he thought at the beginning.

He was lonely, had fallen out with his old girlfriend, and was on the job in a strange city, too new to have any close acquaintances. Wily old Cora recognized his condition and toadied up to him. She loaded his plate with her cooking and extras and invariably passed him the largest piece of pie. She showed concern for his welfare when an occasional overtime assignment delayed his arrival for her rigidly scheduled meals. She would feed him anyway.

And gradually Cora became friendlier. She managed

to brush against him when she leaned over to serve. And she started to tease and ruffle his hair. "You're a good looking fellow, Chester. Why don't you have a lady friend?"

This attention was uncomfortable at the start, but Chester was becoming increasingly edgy. He had only the other day received confirmation through a "Dear John" letter that the back-home affair was over. He was sad and distraught.

One day, looking down to the floor, he noticed Cora's ankles. *They were neatly formed and well designed*. They came up above a delicate foot, surprisingly trim considering the burden they bore.

Chester shook his twenty-year-old head in disbelief that he could find any minute part of Cora in any way attractive and rushed from the dining room and out into the brisk, fresh air to destroy the outrageous thought. Day after day he tried to keep his eyes averted, but inevitably they traveled down from the frowzy tinted hair, the thick goggles and flashing gold teeth, past the sagging breasts and bulging hips, to the shapely ankles.

"They really were neat, those feet, *both of them,*" he thought. "She did have good taste in shoes."

How he managed it, he did not know, but he was in self-disbelief when he heard himself ask Cora if he might visit her bedroom that evening, and with twinkling eyes and a vigorous nod, she agreed.

Late that night Chester crept stealthily down the dark steps in the rear of the house, rarely used by the other boarders. He would have collapsed with embarrassment had he collided with one of them—his contemporaries—at that hour.

A dim light shone under Cora's door. He opened it after a discreet knock. There she was in bed in a frilly pink nightgown, and a lacy pink cap that covered her faux red hair. Her big shiny gold teeth and obviously made-up face and big smile were immediately in evidence. But those titillating ankles were under the covers and nowhere in sight. What had been the focus of his interest was nowhere to be seen. Horrified, he stared in vain, in his search of the stimulus of his desire. *They were not there!* He turned tail and fled. No jack-rabbit could ever have out-sped him that night. He was back to his room in a flash.

The next day, Chester was delayed at work with overtime duties, and no meal awaited him in the unlighted dining room when he returned to the house.

In the darkness he saw the light. He moved to new quarters that next weekend.

Duty, duty, toil and trouble

That damned fortune cookie! It said: "Remain resolute and unwavering when shirking your duty."

That cookie spelled trouble—like when I found a five-
dollar bill at Montgomery Mall. My duty demanded that:

- I should post it in a prominent place with a note
  saying, "Take it only if you can positively identify
  it." And someone would start to take it, and I would
  challenge him, and he would claim it says "In God
  we trust," and I would say it does not because in
  the U.S.A., we believe in the separation of the
  church and state—and he would turn out to be a
  member of the Religious Right.

- Or perhaps I should take it to the nearest FBI office for fingerprints and trace it to its rightful
  owner. But that would take time.

- Or I should stand in the spot where I found it and
  wait for a teary youngster to come by looking for
  the lost bill. His ear would be between his angry
  mother's fingers, pulling him about to find the lost
  money. I would chide her for child abuse, and she
  would haul off and hit me with her umbrella. The
  child would scream even louder, my eye would
  bleed, the place would swarm with security guards,
  and I'd wind up at Suburban Hospital with a
  humongous shiner and a summons to court for
  disturbing the peace. And would Sylvia understand
  when I explain I was hit by an angry woman to
  whom I offered a five dollar bill?

I resolutely shirked my duty and kept the money.

Another time my duty was severely taxed was when the grocery bag carried by a good-looking young woman burst open, spilling dozens of items on the parking lot area. My duty required that I stoop to conquer—I mean to assist in collecting the spillage.

Among the litter were cigarettes, a pound of real butter, and a box of Godiva Chocolates. What would she think if I scooped them up and said, "You are a very foolish woman. The smokes will ruin your lungs, the butter will clog your arteries, and the sweets will give you acne."

She would say it's none of my business, and I will say it's my duty to help her. During the argument, her boyfriend would come along and assume I had assaulted her in some way, and no one would be near who was an expert in conflict resolution. I'd be beaten mercilessly.

So I was firm in my decision. I did not help her in any way and was resolute in shirking my duty.

I'm no fool, you know.

Man with a placard

You have seen the man day after day as he walks on the median strip at the busy intersection in this affluent suburb. He carries an empty Campbell Soup can and a hand-lettered sign on a rough piece of corrugated cardboard. It says simply:

> Out of work
> Please help me

Though his clothes are old and his running shoes ancient, he does not seem dirty or emaciated. He has a generous mustache and a full head of speckled hair and shows no obvious physical handicap. When the cars stop for the red light, he walks as far as he can before the light changes as he hopes for a motorist to drop a coin or bill into the can.

I have watched the expression on his face on successive days, and I have been struck by its blankness. I could not read his mask. His eyes were neutral, his lips mouthed no abusive or pleading words or even a smile. Something is out of whack here, I thought.

Who is he, and why does he make this daily trek for handouts? I can't help it, but my mind plays out various scenarios about him.

It is obvious, you say. The man is unemployed and wants help, you say. I don't think so!

I speculate that he is some sort of a minister of a silent gospel. He wants drivers in their SUVs and luxury cars to see him and examine their consciences as they drive by.

"How lucky I am by comparison," one will think. "Maybe he's too proud to take a low-level job, of which there are many," scoffs another. "Here's a couple of bucks, guy," says a third. "I've been there." A fourth is embarrassed and looks away. A fifth thinks the government must do more for the indigent.

I then wonder if perhaps the "beggar" is a retired college professor and enjoys this uncomplicated life— no hassles over grade inflation, no need to publish or perish, no need to seek grants from government agencies, no stuffy libraries and mold-producing allergies from ivied walls.

I remember that a few years ago, the president of St. John's College worked as a garbage collector for a week to measure the public's attitudes toward those honest workmen.

My curiosity finally got the better of me, and I decided to confront the man. One afternoon I intercepted him on the sidewalk.

"May I buy you lunch?" I ask. "I have watched you work the street and wanted to get acquainted. In my advanced age, I'm a would-be writer and have been imagining all kinds of scenarios about you and your daily activity. I don't think you really want a job and need a handout. That's all really a fake, isn't it?"

There was a foreboding moment of silence as I waited for an indignant or abusive reply, but his eyes lit up, his mouth broadened into a great smile, and he burst out uproariously.

"Thank God for you!" he exploded. "I've spent six months waiting for some intellectually curious and open-hearted person to ask me what I was up to. Not even a cop has stopped to see if I were mentally unstable or somebody who needed some kind of community aid. Let's find a quiet place to eat and talk, and the meal is on me!"

What Cecil (his first name only, please) told me was most exciting, and regretfully I may not reveal too much. He is an inventor and had made millions from his creations, only to have his fortunes and patent rights melted away by unscrupulous business conglomerates. His family and friends had disappeared along with his wealth.

"I was as miserable as a human being can be," Cecil said, "but one day I had a vision of a device I could construct that would revolutionize the way people all over the world could better relate to each other. With my gadget, we could once and forever eliminate the destructive wars that have plagued us from the beginning of time...and make money doing it."

"I have walked the streets since then, quietly working out the details in my mind as I trudged back and forth eking out a modest living. I had just crossed the last 't' and dotted the last 'i' when you approached me. How can I ever reward you for your marvelous introspection and friendly interest?"

We met a few more times, reviewing the details of his invention. Then I thought of a way Cecil could generously reward me, by allowing me part of the action. I happily advanced him a modest amount of funds from my retirement savings.

I am now patiently awaiting his return to the city with his completed plans...waiting...waiting...

Coincidences and miracles

You won't believe this story. After all, I don't write as good as Henry Hemingway or that other fellow Oscar Pyle, but the tale is true, full of miracles and unbelievable coincidences. And it just happened like down the boardwalk at Coney Island.

John Silverstein saw the morning was warm, and he could take a little swim. Halfway down the sand, he remembered he had not left his false teeth in the drinking glass as was his wont, but decided he could get away with a little swim without any trouble. As luck had it, when he opened his mouth wide to alert Mrs. Weinglass that a big wave was coming, his teeth fell out.

Very upset, he notified the lifeguard and asked that he be alert to the chance that the sea would cough up his missing molars.

Now comes one of the coincidences. Hardly 200 yards down the beach, Mrs. Hilton could not wait to walk 20 feet into the ocean to tell Mrs. Friedman that her niece had had a seven-pound baby girl, when that same wave struck her and caused her mouth to pop open and discharge her false teeth!

Like Silverstein, she reported her loss to the other lifeguard farther down on the beach, hoping that somehow they would wash ashore.

Now comes the other coincidence. Both sets of false teeth were recovered a few days later. Some whale must have coughed up Mrs. Hilton's choppers, because she had become accustomed each day to eating gorgonzola sandwiches with a slice of Bermuda onion while watching Oprah Winfry, and the orca found it unpleasant. We have no thesis as to why Silverstein's teeth reappeared.

And now for one of the miracles. Mrs. Hilton's falsies—teeth that is—perfectly fit old Silverstein! And his teeth needed no adjustment in her mouth! Though they were like fingerprints that cannot be duplicated, only God knows how this phenomenon could occur.

I should have told a bit more about these two persons. Mr. Silverstein was a quiet, studious bachelor who preferred to watch football by himself while he contemplated the existential circumstance of two groups of men trying to batter each others' brains out.

On the other hand, Mrs. Hilton, a widow, was a well-known town chatter-mouth, who was the first to know who was having intercourse with whose wife, or vice versa, and how much more rent her neighbor was paying, and how Golschmitch, the butcher, was weighing his thumb along with the meat.

And now the second miracle. With Silverstein's teeth in her mouth, Mrs. Hilton became silent. No hint of a scandal passed her lips. She suddenly became a contemplative, private person. And Silverstein became a chatterbox; nary a hint of a scandal failed to be repeated by him. He was out and about reporting this and that. As you can surmise, the exchange of teeth had a considerable impact on both parties. Who can say for good or bad?

Now the last coincidence. They met eating Sicilian-style pizzas at Papa John's in Brooklyn. His was with sausage and hers vegetarian. Seeing this lovely quiet lady, something familiar in her smile, Silverstein made a pitch for her, speaking eloquently in a way never before possible.

She recognized his fine qualities, his warm, gentle behavior and his eloquence. They met frequently. She had given up gorgonzola and onion sandwiches, and football was too confining for the new Silverstein. Occasionally he fancied the gorgonzola but preferred a clove of garlic to a slice of Bermuda.

Do you know they are now married and sharing a nice piece of property near Sarasota? They call it the Silver Hilton Estates. Do you believe the luck of those guys?

Only in America, as my mother used to say.

Word plays

I have not been able to determine to my satisfaction what there is about fathers and mothers that is embarrassing to their children—I mean normal fathers and mothers.

In my own case, my parents were foreigners with a funny accent, and I wanted very much to disassociate from that alien element. My brothers and I spoke English to perfection and, at least in my case, wanted to shed any taint of the guttural East European transliteration of the American tongue.

I

My wife and I were straight, neighborly, and cooperative in community and school ventures, perhaps more than many, because she played the piano at elementary school functions, and I was active in the PTA. When the school invited parents to back-to-school functions on holidays when the kids had to work but we did not, our daughter's advice on being asked if we should visit her homeroom was invariably, "If you must come, well all right, but promise when you come into the room you won't look at me."

I was a parent who could not be apparent.

When I asked my daughter, now in her forties, if she could remember the cause of her reluctance to be identified with us in a classroom situation, she remembered one occasion. "Mother came to class wearing bobby sox, and while I knew the other girls were envious of me having a mother who would come dressed like a schoolgirl, it was embarrassing."

So her mother was also a parent who could not be apparent. And now you can answer the conundrum: When is a parent not apparent?

II

When is arrival a departure? Well, for one thing, if you and your wife get a prolonged visit from an uncle who said he would disinherit you for marrying out of your faith, that arrival is a departure from his avowed intention.

I had a friend who was entertaining his lady one evening when she bolted upright and cried, "Oh my gosh, I just remembered I told my mother I'd be home at 9 p.m. when my uncle Henry arrives from Seattle. I'll call you tomorrow."

My friend had never heard of her uncle from Seattle. It was not gallant of him, but he followed her at a suitable distance and saw her go into the home of another beau. Her sudden departure was for a rival and his name was not Henry.

So the departure was for arrival at a rival's.

When is arrival a departure?

III

Until I was about eleven, I had not had a birthday party. These events were just not celebrated in the conventional way in our family. I don't mean to say we were neglected, but birthday cakes, candles to blow out and wishes to be made, balloons, pin-the-tail-on-the-don-key, and spin-the-bottle just were not a part of our traditional ways.

Perhaps it was the nature of my parents' business—a candy store with a sideline of toys. We never wanted for ice cream and sweets and toys. More often than not, my father would provide us three brothers with new toys he had for sale as an inducement to other children in the neighborhood to beg their parents for the same.

But I had been to birthday parties of my friends, and as my eleventh anniversary approached, I asked my mother to let me have a party. She shrugged, said something about "such nonsense," but said all right. I was to tell each friend the time and the place and proceeded to contact each child I wanted to attend. And a strange thing happened. Without exception, I was asked if they had to bring presents.

While I sorely wanted to be surprised by gifts, something in me made me say no, they did not have to. Looking back I suspect the other kids did not see how the son of a candy and toy store proprietor could want for any goodies—coals to Newcastle.

To this day I remember the absence of presents. There was no lack of presence, but of presents there was an absence. As I look back at this experience of some 60 years ago, I now remember that Sidney Abramowitz showed up with a handkerchief wrapped in tissue paper. I suppose one should not sneeze at that gift, but it did little to assuage my absence of presents.

All this makes me wonder if I should have invited

only Sidney. I might have missed the others' presence, but the absence of presents would have been easier to take.

Question: Is an absent present better than a present absence? You figger it.

Fortune cookies—bah!

Call me biased, anti-Oriental (even though I have a Japanese daughter-in-law), and a cynic. I even like Fuji apples, but I have lost faith in fortune cookies!

My recent experience with three of them makes me urge you to put no faith in them in prognosticating your future. Here's why. My first one said, "If you can shape it in your mind, you will find it in your life."

I can shape in my mind a plethora of lightly-clad women seated around a room and me in the middle, staring fixedly at one after the other. Just looking. This old man's fantasy (I am sure the many psychiatrists now living among us would tell me) relates to my experience as a child of six or seven.

Early one morning, I knocked on the door to pick up my friend, Sammy, and his mom called me to come in and take a seat at the table while her son got dressed. I did so.

Mrs. Vincent, a big woman in a see-through night-gown, came into the room with the morning paper and took her seat at the table. Then, to my astonishment, she lofted one pendulous breast onto the table and then the other and proceeded to catch up on the news. I stared stunned and wondered what those lightly-covered elephantine objects were. It was weird, if not life-threatening. As you see, I have not forgotten the shock.

I can shape my old man's fantasy in my mind, but where do I go from here to find it in my life and still satisfy, as I must, the second cookie? It said, "Be the first to try something new."

It came with no explicit directions to achieve the advice of fortune cookie No.1. It was gratuitous without instructions, which leads me to cookie No. 3, "Idleness is the holiday of fools."

So here I am in Maplewood Park Place, fantasizing in my idleness with little time to try something new. No bevy of beauties, and no directions. I'm just a fool.

I think I'll stop eating Chinese. That'll show 'em.

Pregnant tale

It wasn't enough that Shelly was pregnant, but this also was the day that one man had to be designated responsible for the plant. Who would it be? How would the others react?

"Talk to them straight," her father, Malcolm, had said sternly. "Speak forthrightly. The situation requires it. But never forget the consequences of close contact."

She now called a meeting of the men with whom she had become involved during the last few months as the

CEO of the company where all had worked for years. The roster included:

- Steffan—straightforward engineer, always available at her call. Dependable but dull, although coming up with surprises in her private sessions with him.

- Eric—now there was a physique—muscular and brainy—he had been a schoolteacher back in Belgium. Had revealed possibilities she had not dreamed of and taught her well.

- Klutz—knew every angle of such private enterprises, ingenious, introspective. But sadly too careless in the intimate detail.

- Will—an astrophysical geological anatomist, an unbelievable illusionist who would be sadly missed in certain situations.

- Spitz—a dogged and faithful midget, or "little person" as they are now labeled, who was underfoot a lot but had made contributions as a minimalist in tight face-to-face activity.

"I cannot claim shame, remorse, or even anger in the delicate situation of which we are all a part," Shelly began. "My father, the president, has been in southwest Africa for several months and finally has found the solution that is right for our situation. In the meantime, as the company's CEO, I have done my level best to get from you what was best. As you must know, the relationship has led to failure, and the plant is virtually bankrupt."

Shelly paused and took time to examine the response

she was receiving at this crucial moment. Steffan was scowling as usual. He has been the most difficult in, shall we say, touchy confrontations. Eric was hard to read, to get a feel for, as cold Norsemen are wont to be. Klutz had his perennial smile. Would he ever get serious? Tall Will was a contradiction in attitudes, every one different. And Spitz, little Spitz, was always ready for anything she might suggest, large or small.

"First I will read from a letter I have just received from my father, Mr. Stingray:"

As you know, I have spent the last few months here in the Congo-Zaire Basin of Central Africa and have finally decided that we must move our plant. It is to a village inhabited by pygmies or as now known, to protect their feelings, forest foragers. They live a few miles from a port on the Oka-Kwongo river, where I have already built a factory after padding a few paws, heh, heh, heh.

I can tell you these people are small in stature but tall in their ability to learn, and since they earn an average of about $54 a year, we can increase that substantially in a short period of time to guarantee their loyalty. These poor folks will experience a vast improvement in their lives.

They are being trained by graduate students from Bangladesh University to handle the macrobiotic equipment the staff has so ingeniously developed in the last 20 years.

The new facility is in their village of Gabonville. Consequently, we will be in a fine position to offer Wal-Mart an even better deal in our products—Sears may even bite the bullet—thus making life easier for U.S. consumers.

Shelly waited a few minutes for the announcement to sink in and then continued, "Before I reveal who will be retained as the responsible one, my father guarantees the rest of you will receive glowing letters of recommendation, and will provide you with a munificent advance in salary of six months, and your health insurance will similarly be extended. These are generous acts, and he and I know you appreciate them." (She thought she heard a grumble.)

"Now for the announcement as to which of you has been chosen to head The North Hampton Assembly Company of Borneo. It is Spitz Dryness we have chosen, not only because Spitz has brought such talent to us, but because in our judgment the pygmies of Southwest Africa will have less trouble looking up to our favorite small man than to any of you others."

"My father said to wish you Godspeed," she concluded, and the men—all but Spitz—were dismissed.

And then the exhausted Shelly went home to her husband.

Matters of perspective

What is a U 2? Is it the second of an **U**ndisclosed experiment in human behavior? Is it another **U**niverse to be explored as an escape from this sorely troubled one in which we now live?

U 2—U 2? We hear it all the time. You say to some-one "have a good day" and the reply is "U 2." You tell someone you have had a rotten day. The reply is a sym-pathetic question, "U 2?" What does it all mean? Is it a sign of conversational deprivation?

You have invited a quirky friend to enliven your party, and he doesn't show up. What's the consequence of the absence of his presence? Is he guilty of mis-prescience? Suppose he shows up absent a present? Is his eccen-tric absence a present? He's been drinking a lot of absinthe lately. Would you say his non-present-absence is because he has become absinthe-minded? Such im-ponderables...

The other day one of two fortune cookies told me, "Nothing is better than happiness, but a ham sandwich is better than nothing." It started me thinking. My fortunetellers had many choices to contrast with the missing happiness. Why would they choose a ham sand-wich, which would be inaccessible to me if I practiced my religion? Thinking about the problem, I have tried to substitute many other food products in the proph-esy—liverwurst—corned beef—pastrami—none of them fit.

The other fortune cookie gave me even more trouble.

It said, "Make sure your words touch your wisdom teeth on the way out of your mouth." My wisdom teeth were yanked years ago.

An agitated woman calls the concierge and says, "You must do something about the man who lives in the apartment across the way. He undresses with his shades up and walks around for hours with nothing on! It's indecent is what it is. He should be evicted!"

"Is he doing it now?" asks the man at the desk. She says no. "The next time he's naked, call and we will bring the security people up to witness his transgressions."

Next day she calls to report the guy is indecently exposed again. The security people rush up look out the window. They see nothing in the apartment across the way. "There's nothing there, lady," they say.

"Of course not, you idiots!" she shouts as she gets up on a chair. "Look at him from here!"

So many imponderables needing so much perspective...

Idle ramblings of a writer

Writer's block is a distressing phenomenon. I have been through it a number of times, like right now, for example, as I recover from some distracting surgery.

Recently a Maplewood resident who had been a successful writer asked me for help. She was in distress and suffering from this writing malady. To try to help her, I wrote and sent her this poem:

Lonely and empty, you sit and you stare.
The blank paper beckons; the space remains bare.
You say, "Nothing, oh nothing, wants to come through."
Well, put down a word: a "hello" or "adieu."
Play with it, stay with it, look at it new.
Glance at its side, or turn it around,
Examine its essence, speak to its sound.
All the time scribbling, in time you will find,
The page will start culling the depths of your mind.

"Culling the depths of your mind?" That's quite a phrase for the process.

As I sit here culling, I remember a conversation with a friend now nearing 90 years of age. "How do you manage to maintain your frenzied activities with no apparent let up?" I asked. "Where do you get the energy to race around as you do: teaching, traveling, creating art works, working in a gallery, keeping your house in repair?"

"Oh, there's no secret to my activity," she replied. "The answer is simple. I was born dead!"

"I was stillborn in a cabin on a farm, miles from a city. No doctor was in attendance. They put me in cold water. They put me in hot water. They swatted my bottom. They breathed into my lungs. They prayed and recited incantations. They wailed and cried out in alarm, and just when they reached the end of their resources and were sure I was dead, I sprang to life."

"Now you know where my energy comes from, and how I can keep up this frenzied pace year after year. I have already been dead and don't have to go through the experience of slowing down and dying again! There's nothing ahead but life and activity."

Open letter on disease control

To Maplewood Park Place Management:

I would like to suggest a plan for eliminating diseases from the dining areas. It calls for a simple procedure at little extra drain on the budget.

The only cost would be for a germ-proof stainless steel box with a pry-proof lid to be positioned in the lobby during months to be designated as Leave Your Diseases in the Box Month (LYDITBOM).

Here's how the plan would work:

At the start of LYDITBOM, all residents would receive cards on which to list all their diseases—not excluding minor ailments like toothaches, in-grown toenails, hemorrhoids, muscle spasms, swollen egos, dented dispositions, running noses and dangling participles. Leak-proof envelopes would be provided with the cards.

All residents would be asked to deposit the envelopes in the box strategically located at the concierge desk and safely away from the food areas. (Concierge attendants fearing contamination would have the option of free inoculations with broad-spectrum antibiotics.)

At the dining tables, residents would be on their honor not to refer to the material dropped into the container. Absolute security must be guaranteed by Maplewood management, and any employee found examining the contents would be summarily dismissed.

LYDITBOM would eliminate disease from the tables and leave diners free to talk of more pleasant happenings—trips, movies, grandchildren, stock-market fluctuations, sporting events, philosophical meanderings about love, politics, and other human degeneracies.

I suggest that great care would have to be exercised periodically to dispose the contents of the box and not leave them festering in the lobby. I have already made preliminary and discreet inquiries to assure safe handling of the noxious materials.

The Montgomery County Board of Health, in cooperation with representatives of the Environmental Protection Agency and the Department of Energy, with advice from the MPP Medical Director, would engage a Wells Fargo armored truck to carry the contents under State Police escort to a reliable disposal location. One possible destination is a site in the Arkansas Ozarks, which in the last six years has become the depository of untold amounts *of political diseases, dirty rumors and scandalous innuendoes.*

I do not expect MPP management to commit immediately to the program. But please think about it. I think the LYDITBOM concept would be copied and adopted quickly throughout the entire corporate retirement community system.

Sincerely yours,
Harry Weiss

p.s. After this program is under way, I plan to suggest another periodic month-long activity, perhaps called FACILEBLAB. A box made of burnished Baobobbian slats, found only in Pago Pago, would contain cards with discussion topics imprinted—such as "My most joyful sex experience," or "The day I was married I discovered one eternal truth," or "I never got to make my own career choice because..." Residents would pick a card randomly and be asked to elaborate on the subject at the dining table. You get the idea, I'm sure.

Sins of the elderly

The most bitter remorse is for
the sins we didn't commit.

When I read that Mexican proverb recently, I wondered how relevant it might be to us here in Maplewood Park Place.

In these days of taking polls for everything, I wondered if the halls of MPP might produce some interesting information about sins, those we committed or wished we had.

Are we beyond the sinning stage or just waiting for a chance? Are we regretful or remorseful about past temptations? Would a random sampling reveal some general conclusions about the subject perhaps suitable for an Ann Landers column?

In my innocence, I soon discovered the subject was risky when I approached a resident who had been an active Washington-area club woman. I thought I knew her well enough to broach the subject. "Oh mercy," she whimpered. "You wouldn't really want me to comment on that, would you?" She fled toward the East Wing elevators.

Another resident with a philosophical flair showed no such reticence. "Yes, I have sometimes felt remorse for having failed to commit certain sins when I have had the clear opportunity to do so."

Well now, I thought, I was getting somewhere. But I was taken aback when I alarmed a former suave military man. He routinely walks out the front door across the neighboring compound for Sunday services. "Will the Monsignor be reading this?" he asked. "I have said enough Hail Mary's and Our Father's for sins I committed not to answer your questions about those I wish I had! No more Rosaries for me, thank you!"

The next man I questioned was a former Foreign Service Officer. "What do you mean, do I regret lost opportunities?" he thundered undiplomatically. "I've still got time, and I think I know someone else here who does too."

"That's disgusting," barked a lady who had been eavesdropping. "I'm going to report you to the MPP standing committee on improper behavior. The idea of asking a question like that! You're violating Article IV, Item 11 of the resident's code of conduct! You should be thrown out!"

Another irate resident asserted that "MPP stands for My Personal Pleasures, and they're none of your damned business!"

I have discontinued my search for other attitudes about the subject of sin in MPP, but perhaps I had a good sampling after all.

If someone had asked me for my own reaction to the proverb, I might have said, "I am neither bitter, remorseful nor regretful, but I still can dream, can't I?"

But then again, I might not have answered at all.

Squeezing the oranges

As I stood poking through the oranges at Magruder's supermarket one day, I recognized the man standing next to me. He had been a top official at the Commerce Department and was also fingering the fruit.

Nudging, I said, "In the end, we all wind up squeezing the oranges, don't we?" We had a good laugh. He had had a national audience for his expertise as an economist, and as a press officer for the agency, I had helped him earn attention. We had not mixed socially, but here we were on the people's ground smelling the melons for ripeness and feeling the plums for edibility.

The experience is a metaphor for the downsizing of our egos, the acceptance of the reality of aging and the leveling of the playing field. We're all in the business of facing our mortality.

As a former lowly yeoman in the U.S. Naval Reserve, I sit comfortably and break bread with a former Admiral or Commodore. The nurse sits easily with the doctor, the liquor salesman with the preacher, the lawyer with the divorcee who hates "those connivers," the practicing Jew with the fervent Catholic with the outspoken atheist. The missing link in this leveling is the lack of members of the less affluent community, but the metaphor holds.

When one day I publicly expressed disdain for the antics of Senator Jesse Helms, someone warned me not to say this if I had dinner with a certain confirmed conservative among us. "He'll bite your head off," she said.

"Bullocks," was my approximate answer. "At my age I'm not about to hide my opinions. Of course I'll be polite, but what am I afraid of?"

I am reminded of a sermon by a Rabbi who told his congregation he was impressed with his relative unimportance in the scheme of things. "In terms of the universe I am miniscule, a nothing, like a drop of water in all the oceans. Humility is required of me."

"I agree with you," said the cantor. "I too feel insignificant. I am a nothing. I am like a cosmic speck in the Milky Way."

Interrupting the two-way sermon, the sexton was impelled to add his two-cents worth. He piped up, "I agree with you both. I am like a grain of dust in this barrel of dirt. I am also a nothing."

The rabbi turned to the cantor and whispered, "Look who thinks he's a nothing!"

There is arrogance even in humility.

For men only (*Women: Do not read*)

Among my many ponderings and wonderings and explorations, I have pondered the differences between old men and women. One of the most significant differences is that of underpants. It is called the backward-forward-availability syndrome.

On occasion, in a foggy moment, an old man will put his underpants on backwards. This is a significant difference because, when next he finds it necessary to go to the bathroom, he becomes profoundly puzzled to discover his equipment is not accessible. He wrinkles his brow, scratches his head and wonders where it has gone?

Now what is the solution to this dilemma? Oh, some younger folks among our readers will scoff and say the solution is easy. "You just be more aware of the two sides of the garment when getting dressed and put it on right!" But that's like telling a deaf man that if he listens more carefully he will discern the difference between "rabbit" and "rarebit" or between "mistake" and "missed steak."

Believe me, I know there comes a time when an old man will put his briefs on backwards. The solution is easy.

I have written to the manufacturers of Fruit of the Loom drawers and also Jockey Shorts and informed them that in this aging population, there is a huge undiscovered market for two-sided men's drawers. Fronts will be backs, and backs will be fronts, and men will be boys again, so to speak. I have even suggested they be called Maplewood Discoveries, because the idea originated with us here at Maplewood. They will put it on billboards that say, "Be happy! Wear Maplewood Discoveries. Your equipment will always be safe with us!"

Now, as to the hearing problem:

I want hard-of-hearing men to start wearing pendants as women do. I am suggesting to manufacturers of costume jewelry that they produce a line of pendants for old men—called wagglers—to waggle if they don't hear something clearly.

These pendants would have illustrations that declare there is a hearing problem. It can picture a duck who says his hearing is down (get it?) or a senator who says he demands a hearing. The old man can waggle the pendant when he misses something in the conversation instead of shouting, "DAMMIT! SPEAK LOUDER. WHAT DID YOU SAY?" and "Huh?"

In this same regard, I am suggesting a line of signs for the hard-of-hearing to put on their front doors to remember their hearing aids when going out in public. The reminders will say, "Are you wearing your hearing aid today? Your friends want you to hear what they have to say."

(Sometimes hearing aids are a nuisance, as when you are dancing cheek to jowl, and the darn things start to whistle. But then again, they can be left off deliberately. That is a sly way of getting close to the lady, and it can be our secret.)

I am also suggesting another poster for the front door that addresses itself to forgetfulness about zippers. In big bold letters it will say: X Y Z. This of course is to remind you to eXamine Your Zipper. It should preferably be in the up position unless, of course, you are trying to find...well, you know.

I am happy to make all of these suggestions in the public interest. After all, as I said in a previous column, I want to do something for humanity. But don't mention a word to the ladies, please.

For Men Only, No. 2

You will recall that I wrote to the manufacturers of men's underpants suggesting they fashion two-sided versions to satisfy a potentially vast old-men's market for their products. Now I have received the following two letters in response to the suggestion:

JOCKEY SHORTS CORP.
WAUWATOSA, WIS.

Dear Mr. Weiss,

At your suggestion, we made 50,000 shorts with two-sided apertures and did a feasibility-marketing study in Wacjasaki County, Minnesota, known for its aging population. After intensive merchandising promotion, we regret to tell you that 38 men and seven women suffered broken legs and mangled hips as they placed their feet into wrong holes and collapsed in a tangled heap. We do not know why women were tempted, for our designs were very macho.

As a result, the U.S. Consumer Products Safety Commission made us destroy all the other Maplewood UnderPants. However, our interest was aroused by the possibility of a new market, and our scientists tried numerous techniques to help older men recognize the fronts from backs of our products.

They included sounding devices like jingle bells and other noise makers attached to the rear, strips of Velcro with warning signs, and even ingenious electronic devices that alerted local fire departments of people tied in underpants knots. We lost several users with dislocated hips in Monome, Montana, and finally gave up after the Western Fraternity of Fire Chiefs complained of too may alarms.

We appreciate any ideas you may have in the future, and you know now what to do with them.

> *Sincerely yours,*
> *Mike Sylvester III*
> *Assistant to the President*

FRUIT OF THE LOOM, LTD.
Malaysia Adjunct

Dear Mr. Hally Wies:

Thanking you for suggestion two side drawers. Pants have four sides in Thailand. What becomes of left side and right side of same. Not much fabric left after four side have openings. Awaiting your solution. We make fine thongs here, 16 cents per hour. Hear soon from you.

> *Sincerely,*
> *Kimbo, chief's cousin*

MEN OF MPP:

I thought you ought
To know the ends I sought
Have come to naught—
That's aught-aught,
And I am distraught.

Catching up to where you were

I looked out the window, and my old friend Dana Moore was walking backwards around the block. He was in shorts and wearing bobby sox. When he came round the second time, I walked out to intercept him. "What are you up to, Dana? Why are you walking backwards?"

"My name is not Dana," he replied. "It's Anad. I am now Anad Eroom."

"When did all this happen and why, Anad?" I asked.

"It's all very simple," he said. "I'm just reversing the aging process. My name change is a help in that direction. I have decided that if I walk backwards from now on, I'll get back to where I was. I have been limited by my lack of speed, but I'm doing much better now than yesterday, thank you."

"Where did you get the idea for this age-diminishing, reverse-direction phenomena?" I asked.

"It's my conception, and you describe it well. I call it ADREDIP—age-diminishing, reverse-direction phenomena. It is well known that if you can travel at speeds greater than the speed of light, you can see history being repeated in deep space."

"Well, recently, when I awoke after being hit on the head by a foul ball at Camden Yards, I realized that to go back in time, you did not have to go into outer space with all the expense of rockets, boosters, space suits, countdowns, ersatz food biscuits, and Tang. You could accomplish it all right here on earth."

"It is simple enough. Just reverse as many of your life processes as you can, and you will become young again."

"What other reversals are you working on?" I asked him.

"Oh, many are available," said Anad. "For one thing, I am having a series of mirrors constructed in close proximity to one another. You know, of course, that when you look into the mirror the person you see is younger than you because of the time lag between your looking and its bouncing back. Well, with enough mirrors you can bounce all the way back to your youth."

"Uh huh," I said. Anything else?"

"Oh yes, much more. You know those bronze shoes your mother always made of your first baby walkers? I discovered they can be de-bronzed and converted back to nice, soft white leather. I'm having mine done. And to help my body along, I'm arranging for liposuction to get rid of all this beer-barrel fat, and I'm having my baby pictures processed and inserted in Madame Lepescu's crystal ball and..."

Just about then a rescue squad vehicle appeared, and two huge medics in white uniforms wrapped Anad in a stylish, chartreuse straitjacket and took him away.

It was an appropriate conveyance. We have all seen in big letters on the front of these vehicles the mirror-image word ECNALUBMA.

It seems appropriate for people practicing ADREDIP.

What is good character?

Where does one really get the motivation to change bad habits? Consultation with a psychiatrist? Reading a how-to book? The three P's—patches, pills or punishment? Good character?

For this essay, let us first establish a few examples of what habits are "bad." Here we will talk about such activities as smoking, drinking hard likker, eating fatty foods to obesity, and peeking into your neighbor's garage to see how he keeps his grass so green, his wife so quiet, and his kids so far away.

I believe we break bad habits out of necessity and that good character has little to do with it, and I am about to cite examples in my own life to prove all of these critical assertions.

Let's start with smoking. When I was a cub reporter, I believed a cigarette had to dangle from my lips, under a snap brim Fedora with a press card sticking in the band. I soon developed a series of sore throats that disappeared when I stopped smoking and reappeared again with the first new puff. Smoke equaled sore throat. No smoke, no sore throat. It hurt. I quit. What's good character about that?

Now drinking: It was graduation eve at college. I was invited with other seniors to a bang-up party in a private home off campus where a chemistry major had made three gallons of his secretly concocted gin. I boldly sampled a thimblefull for starters. I needed no furthers. Sick as a Swiss Weimaraner, I stumbled back to my dormitory room and conked out. Fifteen hours later, I awoke just in time to get my degree, be-gowned and be-shaky and be-gone. A similar experience later proved I cannot drink, hence I do not drink because I get sick. Now what's good character about that?

Let's talk about fatty foods. This confession is hard to make publicly but I will, although it happened here in Maplewood. Several weeks ago I popped a button on my trousers—the top button, which closes and keeps things secure and modest.

Showing ingenuity, I got out my wife Sylvia's sewing basket, chose a (please excuse the expression) stout thread and proceeded to thread the needle. I moistened the end of the thread, but I could not get the thread through the eye of the needle, not even though my father had been a tailor and my mother a seamstress! I was glad they were not alive to witness this break with history.

I procured a magnifying glass, an extra-bright light and a pair of needle-nose pliers. The eye still shimmied, the thread snaked in all directions, and I cussed imaginatively.

Then I got serious. I went to Bruce's all-purpose department store. They had no pre-threaded needles with an array of colors, and so I purchased a needle threader, but I had forgotten how to use it properly. Finally, the wire stretched out and broke.

I cannot abide a waistline that pops buttons off my trousers, so I have had to cut out the sweets. I no longer eat Maplewood Park Place's international desserts, like

French Tiramisu, Florida key lime pie, Belgium devil's food cake, Dutch apple pie, German strudel, Afghan rhubarb tarts, American Oreos, ice cream, Boston cream pie, or Armenian strawberry mice swimming in a chocolate cup. Even one mousse and my buttons pop. My corporeality is showing, and I am dieting. Now what's good character about that?

My wife says letting a popped button send me screaming to Bergmann's Laundry for help is perfectly consistent with my past behavior. Didn't I once trade in a perfectly fine Volvo because my right rear-view mirror broke, and it would cost $30 to replace it? It was easier to trade it in for a $30,000 Mercedes Benz. Now that's good character.

So, by the way, is my not talking about the neighbor's wife.

Pills, pills, pills

I don't mean to make you envious or anything, but I now take 12 pills a day—one dozen!

I once hated to take even one pill. I thought it was brave to spurn an aspirin even for a headache. When the dentist suggested Novocaine before drilling a tooth, I denied him the pleasure. I even refused painkillers when I had my tonsils removed. Oh, what a macho lad I was! No sissy me! No sir-ree.

But all that has changed. My doctor put it this way: "How would you ever have gotten to be 88 if it were not for the wonderful pharmaceuticals I have been pushing down your throat for the last dozen years?"

He equates my longevity to the drugs, though my father managed to reach the mid-90s without them. I even recited this, my poem, to him with no effect, not even a titter:

> *Longevity is a wondrous trait*
> *Acclaimed in verse and song,*
> *And everyone can reach that state,*
> *If they only live so long!*

Let me tell you about these 12 little varmints he has made me take. I start with three for blood pressure. Pink goes to work when the pressure is too high. Yellow kicks in when it is too low, and the chartreuse adjudicates between the two. They put their little heads together and somehow work things out right.

Now let's go to the irregular heartbeat and the minor aortal block. The blue-and-yellow capsule calculates the frequency of missed beats on its abacus. The mauve waits for instructions and tells the sunset peach when to kick in. I don't know how those little critters do it. How do they know where to go in this vast territory of 157 pounds? It really beats me.

Meanwhile, my pacemaker has been standing by— my second one in 10 years—to see if all six critters have come up with the right decisions. Good old pacemaker— I'll let you feel the bump on my chest if you are a friend.

A little purple capsule looks after my hiatus hernia.

That little bugger has been so successful I can now eat that big fat Hebrew National kosher hot dog with catsup and piccalilli without my stomach barking and meowing and doing the Mexican chop-chop.

That now leaves five pills. We won't detail what they are for. The fact is that I am extraordinarily healthy. Sylvia reminds me of that every day. (Grr-rr-rr). She won't let me complain or look for the symphony I deserve. You know, something tuneful, sad and understated, in the key of A-flat.

I now take those five willingly. But even as I am now happily regressing to my childhood, I will not add another pill to the list. Thirteen is notoriously an unlucky number, and it is not for me!

No, no, Doc, please...

The view in retirement

From the lonely windows of creeping age,
The vehicles roll by as life has ridden by.
From whence? The various roles are hidden by
The daily darkening of life's stage.

In the blackness one thinks "careers,"
The shifting gears of upward choice,
The fear function of the boss's voice,
Or downward drag of labor's drears.

Red, yellow lights flash by: to what end the pace?
From dawn to dusk, what goals we face?
At end, what reward justified the race?
Respect? Renown? Family? Beauty? Grace?

Pushing Ninety

One evening I was eating with a couple of residents here at my retirement home, and one asked me how old I was.

"I'm 88," I replied.

"EIGHTY-EIGHT!" they responded with surprise. "YOU ARE PUSHING 90! WHY, YOU ARE AN OLD MAN!"

Until that moment I had not considered myself an old man, though they were just having a little fun. Was I an old man? I now had to do a little research. Was I an old man just because I was "pushing" 90?

Lately I had been napping a lot and attributing it to some new medication the doctor had prescribed. Was that the truth, or could I really be old? I asked another resident of similar age if he too had been napping a lot.

"Of course," he said. "I worked for fifty years, standing on my feet much of the time, and now I do a little, then sleep a little, do a little and sleep a little, all day long. That's called 'retirement.' Do a little, then sleep a little. I love it!"

I decided to confine my research just to the men here, because women might be more touchy on the subject. So I started to stop Maplewood men and ask two simple questions: 1) "Do you consider yourself an old man?" and 2) if so, "Just when did it occur to you that you were old?" Here are some of the interesting answers I received:

The first moment I knew I was old was...

- When I had to give up driving and now depended

on others.

- When my big toe got sore, and my doctor said it was gout. All my life I had seen pictures of old English lords with gout in a easy chair with one lavishly wrapped foot hanging out there.
- When, too many times, I crossed the room to get something and couldn't remember what I went for when I got there.
- After a few years of associating here at Maplewood with old and slow-walking people, I began to know I too was one of us, old and slow-walking.
- When my wife died, and I realized I would have to take care of myself. She wasn't supposed to die before me.
- I started to say something flirtatious to a young woman, and she took my arm and walked me across the street. I hadn't even planned to cross it.
- When, without asking, the person at the ticket counter gave me the senior discount.
- It was when friends around me began to die.
- When the woman on the elevator insisted that I get off first.
- When, at 91, I had to give up tennis!
- When I looked in the mirror.

Should I add when I was "pushing 90?" As Jack Benny said, when a crook demanded his money or his life...I'M THINKING, I'M THINKING...

Part Two.
Slices of a Life

Figure 4. Newsman Harry Weiss attends a press conference.

My brush with history

It has occurred to me, as I near the end of my tour of duty in these climes, that inadvertently I have been a witness to, or a low-level participant in, many of the most significant happenings in the 20th Century.

To start with, I saw my father hauled away in a paddy wagon for selling whiskey by the drink during Prohibition—the infamous and repealed *Volstead Act*. I also saw him carried away in an ambulance with the flu during the great Pandemic of 1918-1919.

Norman Thomas was the first presidential candidate for whom I voted, as a teenager, in the voting booth with my blind brother. That same brother had one of the first seeing-eye dogs in the country—a female German shepherd named Zenta.

One day, as my other brother and I were driving along a dirt road in our Durant automobile near Huntington County, New Jersey, in 1932, we were suddenly surrounded by state troopers with drawn guns. We were frisked, made to remove the bass viol we were carrying and watched as they stripped its cover and peered into its *"S"* holes to see if it contained *Charles Lindbergh's missing baby,* who had just been kidnapped.

On December 7, 1941, I had just arrived in the newsroom of the Cleveland *Plain Dealer* when the AP, INS, and UPI all began to bang out news of the *Pearl Harbor* attack.

One of my assignments was to follow *Eleanor Roosevelt* around Cleveland in case she might be assaulted. I worked for the War Relocation Authority and visited one of the camps where America shamed itself by confining all the West Coast Japanese—a black mark on our history.

A close friend spent the war in jail as a conscientious objector, successfully fasted to get unfair prison rules changed, and another friend headed the American Friends Service Committee and fought against *Nixon* and the *Vietnam War*.

From the balcony of the Department of Commerce, I saw police breaking up an *anti-Vietnam War demonstration* around the Washington Monument.

I saw *Harry Truman* return to the White House victoriously in 1948. I wrote some short messages for him.

Before her marriage to Jack Kennedy, *Jacqueline Bouvier* came into my office, and we had a chat. I stood 25 feet from *President Kennedy* as he waited to be introduced at an affair for which I had handled the publicity.

I shook hands and had my picture taken with *Lyndon Johnson*. I was in the presence of but refused a chance to shake hands and be photographed with *Richard Nixon*. I heard the feckless *Herbert Hoover* tell a group of high-level government workers that they were a nonproductive lot. I received a Silver Medal from the hands of *Franklin Delano Roosevelt, Jr.*, son of the president, who was our Under Secretary at Commerce. While there, he was directed by the president to chaperone

Jacqueline on a visit with *Ari Onassis,* whom later she married and divorced.

My daughter worked at St. Elizabeths Hospital and saw *John Hinckley, Jr.,* would-be assassin of *President Ronald Reagan.* My son was an Air Force captain during the *Vietnam War.* Showing my independence as a voter, I once voted for *Spiro Agnew.*

When the *World Trade Towers* were being built, Secretary of Commerce Luther Hodges and I visited the site and were whisked 110 stories above ground. Iron girders that later melted under the September 11, 2001, terrorists' attack were all that stood between us and the horizon over New York City.

At a meeting called to talk about all the Commerce Department was doing for the black community, a young black man with bushy hair arose and said, "With due respect, sir, what you have told us is a bunch of bullshit." His name was *Marion Barry*, later to serve as the mayor of Washington, D.C. That time, he was right.

A friend was interrogated, and a fellow I knew was victimized by *Senator Joseph McCarthy* and later killed in a prison fight. I was friendly with a neighbor who later was publicly identified as a Communist cell member.

I slightly knew the sculptress Mrs. Letelier, whose husband *Orlando Letelier* was assassinated in Washington on orders from the Chilean government. As an enamellist, I made a Cloisonné pendant for her. I designed and sold a pendant to Mrs. George McGovern, whose husband *Senator George McGovern* ran for Presi-

dent in 1972. I worked as a volunteer for Common
Cause, whose founder *Ralph Nader* probably caused the
defeat of Vice President Al Gore for president in 2000.

I worked personally with lesser lights, such as Lewis
Straus, Maurice Stans, Averill Harriman, Luther
Hodges, and Governor Leroy Collins.

I heard Straus, former Atomic Energy Commission
chairman and disgracer of H-bomb hero *Robert
Oppenheimer*, smear *Washington Post* cartoonist
Herblock. I was asked to change the biography of Commerce Secretary Maurice Stans, the convicted money
collector for President Nixon, from being "a big game
hunter" to "a wild animal conservationist." Others en-
countered in the course of my career included movie
star *William Powell*, the "cowardly lion" *Bert Lahr*, *Pearl
Bailey*, and some Metropolitan Opera stars. I saw *Bobby
Feller* pitch.

Finally, one day after we moved to our retirement
home, I was swimming in the pool with a large man
who spoke to me of having had considerable experience in the military dealing personally with the likes of
President Nixon and *Emperor Hirohito*. I thought he was
some old coot hallucinating and checked him out with
Google on the Internet.

He was telling the truth. He turned out to be *Admiral Thomas Moorer*, the top military commander of the
whole kibosh and caboodle under Nixon.

Thereby hangs my tale.

My $10,000 ad lib

In the years when air conditioning was available in the Department of Commerce only in offices occupied by presidential appointees, notices were routinely sent to all personnel saying that with summer approaching, it was OK to work in short-sleeves, so long as their appearance was neat.

The routine notices were always signed by the Assistant Secretary for Administration. That official in the Eisenhower years was James Worthy of Chicago, a former top executive with Sears Roebuck & Co.

One day shortly after the notice was sent around, Associated Press reporter Frank Cormier came into my office where I was in charge of the news division and asked if there was any news worth reporting. There was none, but I tossed him the hot-weather memo and said, "Maybe this is a story. Jim Worthy sent out this notice and says that the Eisenhower years will be a-roll-up-your-sleeves-and-get-to-work administration."

Next morning virtually every newspaper, radio, and television newscast in the country and some overseas carried my ad lib in Mr. Worthy's name. Somewhat nervously I awaited his call, and it finally came late in the afternoon.

He greeted me with a broad grin and a vigorous handshake. "You know, I have spent the day receiving congratulatory calls from everywhere. I have heard from friends who have been out of touch for years, and best of all, I have just hung up from a call by the President himself—Dwight D. Eisenhower."

He paused a moment and smiled. "Is there anything at all that I can do for you to show my thanks?" he asked.

For some time I had hoped to win a free parking place in the Commerce Department's courtyard in the slightly exaggerated belief that my job required instant availability at all hours. "It would be a great help," I told him.

The next morning, a sheltered spot was assigned to me, and I had it for 20 years until my retirement. I did some rough calculations recently and figured that ad lib had saved me $10,000 in parking fees.

My Mom's priorities

My father was a timid man. The sight of suffering or blood sent him into a tizzy. If he cut his finger, he would shake with fear. It was certainly predictable for him then to rush into my bedroom hysterically one night when I was 14 and shake me awake.

"Harry, Harry, quick, get up and go next door and get Mrs. Leon. We need her help. Your mother is very sick. Hurry, hurry, we need her help."

I jumped out of bed and ran into the living room after my father. Mom was slumped in a chair, her head flat on the table. She appeared to be unconscious, her eyes closed, her arms limp, her face a deathly green pallor. She had passed out in the time my father had come to fetch me.

Seeing her in this worsened condition he shouted, "Oh my God, she's dying, she's dying! Hurry, get Mrs. Leon." And then Pop fainted to the floor.

With both my parents seemingly unconscious, I frantically pulled open the door and streaked down the hall in my underwear. The Leons lived in an adjoining apartment a long corridor away. As I neared their door I heard my mother's voice.

"Harry, Harry," she cried. "Come back, come back." Wondering what that was all about, I turned around and hurried back.

My mother, who had appeared to be deathly ill, raised her head and in a weak voice said, "Harry, Harry. First put on your robe and slippers." Then she passed out again.

It was a transient illness. She lived another 70 years and died in her mid-80s. For all his squeamishness, Pop outlived my mother and passed away in his early 90s.

End of an affair

Like all of these affairs, this one started with unquestioning love; no holds barred. Our needs, all of them, were quickly met, the slightest discomfort responded to, the little hurts quickly repaired, and accommodations to the other's changing moods promptly made. Pride and admiration and warmth marked the days...and the nights.

As time went on, we grew together, making those adjustments required by changing conditions. Sometimes one or the other of us changed reluctantly. Sometimes, a little pressure was required—a sharp word or even a push of sorts.

But people are individuals, and personalities need room to grow, and clashes need to arise to test the strength of one's opinions or feelings, and adjustments to each other become more difficult. And a gap between us began to widen gradually, and a rift became a cleft, and a cleft became a chasm.

Words did not crawl between us; they flew. The moments of quiet talk became increasingly rare. Exchange of opinion was replaced by crossfire or negation. An invisible barrier seemed to grow between us, occasionally shattered by the light of understanding but more usually deliberately kept hanging, because one of the partners felt they could not afford to give in to the other and maintain their self-respect.

In recent days, it was more like an armed truce, no barbed wire or guns at readiness, but eyeball hostility. Efforts at levity misfired; gropings to close the gap were misunderstood.

It was evident that only a divorce would solve the dilemma of two poorly relating parties after 18 years of close association. So on an early Sunday morning, we drove to the airport for the parting, silently, both of us glad to resolve the conflict, get it over with, and restore peace to the establishment—hopefully, anyway.

I watched as the departing figure grew distant on

the ramp to the airplane. And then, as my last son turned the corner on his way to college in New Orleans, I cried like a baby. It was the end and a beginning.

My Navy daze

I was the father of two young children and 29 years old when I was drafted into military service.

As I stood in line about a dozen men back from the Army induction table, someone tapped my shoulder. It was a Cleveland police detective about whom I had once written a favorable story in the Cleveland *Plain Dealer.* He just happened to be passing through the Armory.

"Do you really want to get into the infantry?" he asked. "Hell no," I replied. "I'm not cut out for field rations and all that marching stuff. I'd much rather be aboard a comfortable ship!" He walked over to the Navy recruiting table, which showed little sign of activity, leaned over and whispered to the guys while pointing to me.

Just as I reached the Army desk, a Chief Petty Officer took me by the arm and walked me to his station, where I was enrolled immediately as an able-bodied seaman in the U.S. Naval Reserve. By the end of the day, I was chosen to lead a group of about 20 young recruits by train to the Great Lakes Naval Training Center outside of Chicago.

The Navy wasted no time in depriving me of any claim to individuality. We had hardly alighted when a CPO

Figure 5. Sailor Harry Weiss.

stuck his face into mine. For years I had worn a modest little mustache to give me maturity as a newsman.

"When we get to the barracks," he shouted, "I'll give you 10 minutes to get that shit out from under your nose!" Hours later, I suffered the further indignity of having my hair shorn to virtual baldness with an electric clipper. (I had always thought my curly locks were my most distinguishing feature.)

I spent the next few weeks trying to absorb new basic skills—long marches at a cadenced pace; firing a rifle, while prone, at a stationary target; identifying silhouettes of fast-moving fighter planes; dousing dense smoky fires in the hull of an imitation aircraft carrier; digesting crude foods in overcrowded mess halls; and learning how to swim in ocean waters covered with oil slicks.

The last experience sent me to sick bay with a fever and a very sore throat. I was appalled when, after a long wait, three corpsmen came in from a softball game prepared to treat us. They were hot, sweat-soaked and unwashed. I was even more shocked when one of them used a tongue depressor on one patient and then turned it over and used it again on another! Didn't they know that Great Lakes had been fighting a scarlet fever epidemic?

I was given pills and recovered. A week or so later, I learned that an Antioch College professor, whom I had known, was a lieutenant commander in charge of educational programs at boot headquarters. To renew acquaintances, I called him, and he invited me to breakfast at the officers' mess. What a treat! Fresh eggs, bacon, orange juice, hashed-brown potatoes, choice of breads, rolls and butter and jelly, and freshly brewed coffee. In my memory, it is the best meal I ever tasted.

In the course of a friendly chat, I described the conditions I had found at sick bay. "Maybe that's why they have been unable to lick the scarlet fever that has been raging here," I said.

He apparently lost no time in reporting my conversation to the medical commander. It triggered an inquiry that caused me, the lowliest of seamen, to be summoned to headquarters for a hearing to describe the medical conditions I had seen. I was uncomfortable, and the interrogation by a medical officer was not friendly.

"Are you a doctor?"

"No, sir."

"Have you had medical training?"

"No, sir."

"How do you know they failed to wash their hands? Did you examine them? Weren't they carrying other tongue depressors in their blouses? Where were you standing? Were you in any position to judge? What was the name of the corpsman? Do you have any witnesses who can verify your story?"

He was obviously more intent on discrediting me and protecting his corpsmen than facing the problem of unclean procedures. The commander in charge told me I would hear from them again. As I slunk out of the hearing room to return to quarters, one of the corpsmen whispered, "You bastard. Just you wait 'til the next time you get sick, buddy..."

I was never called back to any hearing and, of course, sick or not, I deliberately avoided any further contact with the health services until my departure from boot camp. Later I learned that the epidemic had subsided, and I like to think that just maybe I had something to do with it.

Who's mettlesome? Not me!

Sure, you might call me a three-metal man. I have three of them—three metals, that is. The first—the World War II medal—was given to everyone who served honorably in the Naval Reserve. It acclaims freedom from fear or want and freedom of speech and religion.

I served where I was sent, which in this case was to a high-rise building in mid-Chicago, where I wrote about the activities of the men in the fleet from information sent by Navy correspondents with the ships at sea.

The second medal I must in all modesty call the "chutzpah" medal. That word means "you gotta lotta nerve" in Yiddish and has been adopted into the English language. While I deserved the award for my contributions to the U.S. Department of Commerce for 25 years (I say shamelessly), it came about in an unusual way.

One day, thinking positively about my work performance, I said to my boss, "You know, I think I deserve a medal for the good work I have done here."

Figure 6. Franklin Delano Roosevelt, Jr. (left)
presents Harry Weiss with a Silver Medal.

"OK," he replied without hesitation. "Go write your-self a citation." So I wrote the citation, stating without fear of being contradicted, that I was a good guy and had served my agency well and had kept it out of trouble, etc. etc.

Several months later, I was told to attend a celebra-tion in the crowded Department auditorium. On the platform stood Franklin D. Roosevelt, Jr., our under secretary. He called out my name, and he read a finely written citation that I was a good guy and had served my agency well and had kept it out of trouble, etc. etc., and he presented me with a Silver Medal. The audience applauded. The best part was that my wife, afflicted with cancer, was proud of me, not knowing how I had engi-neered the whole deal. She died not long afterwards.

A third piece of metal I still have is my dog tag. When I was drafted, the Navy CPO who signed me in asked me what church I went to. I said I did not go to church. So my dog tag has a big "P" on it. He had not asked for my ancestry, which was Jewish. He just assumed that if you were not a churchgoer, well, of course you were a Protestant.

Had I died in the service there would have been a cross over my grave instead of a Star of David. The sky would have darkened, lightning would have flashed over the firmament, the earth would have shaken and shud-dered, and there would have been hell to pay under the sod where I lay.

Memorable quotes

One Maplewood Park Place resident remembers meeting my classical musician brother Bill about fifty years ago. He took her hand in his and said, "What beautiful fingers you have." She never forgot it. It prompted me to recall memorable quotes from my past.

As college magazine reporter, I interviewed Alan Ashley, an African-American. The college had just named a new building Ashley Hall to honor his lifelong services as a maintenance man. "Do you have any special words of advice for this year's seniors?" I asked him. "I have for the men," he responded, "Never tell a woman nothing that you don't want her to remind you of ten years from now. She'll remember it, and she'll tell you."

A world-renowned chemist told me how he had made his career choice. On receipt of his Ph.D., he had two job offers—a high-paying job with the Swift Packing Company and a teaching spot at a prestigious university. "The meat company paid my way to Chicago. They gave me an extensive tour of the slaughterhouse—from the screaming animals in the corral to the packaged meats. That experience unsettled my stomach and settled my mind. I decided to teach!"

It was a drenching rain in downtown Washington. As I started to enter a bookstore, I saw Pearl Bailey coming up behind me. "Aren't you Pearl Bailey?" I croaked, awed by her presence. "I won't be much longer," she retorted, "if you don't let me in out of the rain!"

As a reporter for the *Plain Dealer,* I was assigned to

follow First Lady Eleanor Roosevelt around Cleveland. Another reporter was to write about what she might say, so I asked the city editor what he wanted me to do. "Don't do a thing," he said, reflecting the oft-expressed hostility toward her in those days. "I just want you there if we get lucky, and someone throws a tomato at her!"

I sat in a car in front of a well-known politician's home from four p.m. 'til midnight, instructed to ask if it was true that he was about to marry a showgirl half his age. When he finally arrived, I confronted him. "Don't believe everything you hear," he said and added, "But there's many a slip 'twixt cup and lip." I had nothing to report, but the next day he married her.

As I boarded a plane for a red-eye, night-long, cross-country flight to Washington, I walked right behind the pilot as he entered the cabin. "Would you like a cup of coffee?" the solicitous stewardess asked him. "No thank you," he replied. "Coffee always keeps me awake!"

One day I recognized the "friendly" Wizard of Oz lion, Bert Lahr, standing in front of the National Theater. Impulsively, I approached him. "How does it feel, Mr. Lahr, to have people come up to you and ask silly questions?" His reply was appropriate and instantaneous, "Piss off, kid, you're bothering me."

My wife Sylvia once heard a loud, plaintive voice over the din of the locker room at the clubhouse. "God forbid you should have a day off from worrying." It was a great line, and I used it successfully in several enamels.

As I walked along a northeast Washington street toward my apartment one day, I saw a tiny woman bent over pulling weeds out of her flower garden. To make pleasant conversation as I passed her, I said, "Hello there. What's the news?" With no hesitation, she replied, "Baby shit and had no shoes." Her high laughter followed me to the end of the block.

Pasta with a little origami, please

One day I read an obit in *The Washington Post* about Augusto. For over 40 years, he had been the owner of an Italian restaurant in downtown Washington, D.C.

I once ate in his bistro. It was at a time when I was in my heyday as an origamist—a creator of original paper folds—who had been published in Japan, England and the U.S. A friend, who had invited me to lunch, called Augusto over to our table.

"This man is a magician," my friend said, pointing to me. "He can take an ordinary piece of paper and in a minute, fold a dog, a cat, an elephant, a boat, anything you can name."

"Ha, ha, ha," responded Augusto. "You a big kidder. You always make with the big joke."

"No, no, I mean it," my friend said, knowing I could not resist showing off my skill, and added, "Just get him some paper and see for yourself."

Reluctantly, Augusto brought over a handful of paper menus that I tore into squares. Soon, to his delight and that of many of the other diners, animals of all kinds lined the checkered tablecloth: a cat, a dog, a mouse, a bull, a chicken, an elephant, assorted birds that flapped their wings, and a frog that promptly hopped into the sugar bowl.

"Bravo, bravissimo, these are fantastic," Augusto shouted. "Can I please have them? Please. I am appreciating it very much."

I said sure, of course he could.

"And do you know what I'm gonna do with them?" he asked. "I'm gonna take them home and show them to my seven-year-old kid. I'm gonna show him all these things. Then I'm gonna slap his face good, and I'm gonna say, 'See what some seven-year-old boy made in my restaurant today? Why can't you be smart like him?' "

Reading Augusto's obit these many years later, I was tempted to call his son and tell him the naked truth. It was I, a 45-year-old man, who had produced the menagerie, not a seven-year-old boy. His father had lied to him. But I did not telephone. Let the old man rest in peace, I thought.

Besides, I fantasized, maybe this type of encouragement had succeeded beyond all expectations, and the kid was now a famous brain surgeon. Or on the other hand—shudder, shudder—maybe Augusto had failed miserably. Maybe, in his enthusiasm, the slap had caused the boy serious brain damage.

Had he become a genius or an idiot? I never found out.

Conquest at The Twin Pines

After many months of grief and loneliness following my first wife's death, I found an ad in *The New York Times'* travel section to be very appealing. It promised fun and games for singles in a lodge in the Adirondacks.

I made a reservation, and a week later I pulled into The Twin Pines' parking area. I momentarily panicked. Scores of very young women were alighting from a Greyhound bus. Brightly clad in summery sports togs, they looked as if they had been cloned in the "Young Attitudes" section of Bloomingdale's department store.

But I felt confident I could share in the activities despite my recent sorrow and the obvious generational gap. At that evening's mixer, I approached a young woman and asked if she would like to dance. "Oh, I don't dance," she said. Not far away, a petite brunette said she did not dance either. Others told me they were "just looking," and I marveled at my special instinct for choosing non-dancers. I decided I would just stand and observe.

Of course, I soon discovered that the women who had turned me down were out there dancing with younger men. Their terpsichorean torpor had been induced by my age, but I decided it was nothing personal. They did not want to start their hard-earned and much anticipated week being seen dancing with an older man. The competition for young males precluded any normal courtesies to the aging. I wondered, however, if this R&R center for my re-entry into life was more likely to be D&D—Difficult and Disastrous.

Events turned out better than I had feared. When, in a day or two, pairings had shaken down and become more or less fixed, I was able to find an occasional dance partner. I ate my meals with the same group of nine assigned to the table—among them a grammar school teacher, a waitress, an insurance salesman and Irving, a taxi driver from Brooklyn.

As a government official from the nation's capital, I was something of a hit. In that company I was a towering intellect, telling inside stories about Washington. I had also demonstrated my skills as an origami expert, a skillful folder of paper animals. Much impressed, Irving quickly adopted me as his special charge.

Whenever I passed him on the playing fields, on the trails, in the gym or game rooms, he insisted on introducing me to his companions of the moment. "I want you should meet Harry," he'd say. "He's a real genius. Tell them something, Harry." I would tell them "hello" and walk away as quickly as I could.

At meal times, Irving took pains to see that I wasn't neglected, passing the bagels and pickled herring and delectable desserts to me ahead of the others. I had once heard him whisper, "Harry desoives the best. His wife just passed away, you know."

The week moved quickly, and we were finishing the final meal when Irving rapped for attention. "I want to make a statement as we enjoy this feast together and are about to take our final joineys back to the walks of life," Irving began. "I am soitin you will all agree wit' what I must say on this auspicious occasion. I want to make this announcement, because this is the way I feel in my heart."

"This announcement has to do with one of the members of dis round table, and I want to share it," he went on, then looked squarely at me and asked, "Harry, I want to say something about you. Do you mind? I hope you don't mind. Harry, do you mind?"

Helplessly I nodded assent.

"OK. Here is what I wanna say. For a week, for almost seven days in fact, dis here week, we have sat in dis dining establishment listening to your woids of wisdom. You are so smaht, and watching you fold dem paper things, dose origamis, is too wonderful to mention. I hope you don't mind that I have taken some, because the people in my cab would never believe it when I tell them. See (reaching in his pocket), I have here your chicken [it was a robin], a bunny [it was a dachshund], a horse [it was a fallen fawn] and a box [he got that right]."

He took a thoughtful breath and continued, "And Harry, here is what I have to say. I have never hoid or known any human being with such talent, and so refined, and even so beautiful as you, and I am sure dese friends share with me dese deep feelings. So now we are about to leave this Gahden of Eden for our important woik in the city, I wanna say for all of us, we appreciate your friendship and all you have shared with us."

Ah, at last he was through. He clapped his hands in tribute, and the others joined in. *But he was not finished.*

"And Harry, Harry, I wanna say just one thing more.

Can I say it, Harry, can I?"

Could I have stopped him? I nodded in agreement.

"Harry, wid your brains and my yout' we could conquer the woild!" With that, Irving came boldly around the table, gave me a hug and a resounding kiss on the cheek.

In spite of the odds against it, I had made a conquest at The Twin Pines!

How I lost a million dollars

About a year after my wife's death, I received a letter from my friend Lillian suggesting I might want to get acquainted with a widow whom she knew and could recommend.

Until then, no one had in any obvious way tried to suggest a promising companion. I had begun to strike out on my own, largely through the Parents Without Partners organization. In the club were more than 1,000 women of every age, condition, and level of separation and receptivity. The field was wide open with possibilities for me—a vigorous fifty-year-old government official with a good job, a house, and a decent reputation.

However, I could not ignore Lillian's letter. She and I had had a long association through our interest in origami. What could it hurt if I looked up this "interesting" widow?

I phoned the lady—Sophie—and she invited me over for coffee and cake, for she had already been alerted to the call. She lived in a good part of Washington, in a large, attractive home, richly furnished including deep oriental rugs. Her late husband had owned a very successful wholesale liquor distributorship.

The evening was pleasant enough. She was moderately attractive. Her eyes, nose and other parts were in the right places, and she spoke reasonably well. I thanked her for an enjoyable evening and suggested that we might go to the movies sometime soon.

Hardly a week passed before Sophie invited me to dinner. She was having a few people in the next Saturday, she said, and thought I would like to meet them. My antenna quivered nervously a bit, but I accepted the invitation. So, dressed casually, I arrived at her door for dinner.

The "few people" turned out to be four couples, all blood- or marriage-related to Sophie. The impeccably dressed men were in business suits and were smoking fat cigars. The women were richly jeweled and had an aura of haute couture about them.

As we men nursed cocktails, they told me they enjoyed access to the best golf clubs in Washington, Baltimore and Philadelphia, where some lived. (I had never played golf.) They were in liquor, merchandising, construction. They had places in Florida. They tried to impress me with their ability to get anything at wholesale— "You want automobiles, TVs, appliances, we can get them."

Then dinner was served. It was an elegant catered meal with French-dressed waitresses. A different wine was served with each course. (I was never much of a drinker.) It all overwhelmed me.

A habitually informal guy, I was uncomfortable and out of the loop in the conversations around the table. After dinner, as we sat around in a circle, my discomfort got so intense that I abruptly rose and told Sophie I had to leave. "What's the matter, don't you feel well?" she asked. I told her I felt fine, had enjoyed the meal, but it was time to go. I waved half-heartedly to the other guests, who seemed rather puzzled—the evening was still young—and I beat it.

I did not call Sophie again, but about a year later she called me. "I'm getting ready to move to Florida," she said, "but I couldn't leave the area without asking you why you never called me again. You left the dinner suddenly. Can you tell me what was wrong?"

I explained as honestly as I could that I had not had a chance to know her before she had put me on exhibition with her relatives for a judgment, either about how I felt about her family or they felt about me.

"From my point of view, Sophie, they were not the kind of people with whom I had much in common, and I did not want to be judged by them." After a moment of silence the line went dead.

That's how I lost my chance to be a millionaire.

My solipsism is showing

Some curious events are taking place in my life. I seem to be reverting to my childhood, and I can't help it. Since my actions involve my relationships here at Maplewood, I'm asking for your understanding in advance of these confessions.

When I was a mere lad, I knew the world revolved around me. Every event I experienced took place only in my presence, in a limited circumference around my body and myself. There was no "out there" out there, if you know what I mean.

What I saw moving in the world only moved within the orbit of my eyes. The smells I smelled did not exist when my nose and I left the area. Noises and rackets were only what my ears picked up; out of my earshot was only silence. The temperature I felt was only in a cocoon that accompanied me where ever I went. Only I experienced reality; there was nothing else.

Many times I tested these feelings of uniqueness—that all things existed only as I experienced them. Often as I walked along the street, I would whip my head around to see if the traffic had stopped once I was beyond it. But I could never move fast enough to find the pedestrians frozen in their tracks, the wings of birds stilled in their flight, and the entire horizon rigid and unmoving.

After much effort and many tests, I decided regretfully that I could never twist fast enough to prove that I was the center of the universe. I somehow accommodated to this bitter truth and decided privately just to enjoy the uniqueness that was mine.

But I am now in my dotage and wondering if perhaps I was right in my youthful egocentric beliefs. For example, when I snap my head around now at Maplewood, every one is moving as before, but more slowly. Most are just creeping. I have almost caught them at a stop! What as a child I had imagined as cessation out of my presence is now deceleration. The world isn't stopping, but it seems to be going in that direction...slowing down.

There have been other curious developments. When I see small groups of residents gathered in the corridors, I know they have assembled for me, and I apologize for being late to the meeting.

When someone leaves my presence, perhaps for a trip to the bathroom, they are leaving because of something I said, even when I have been silent. When people noiselessly pass me by, I ask them not to go away mad.

No one reads my articles or laughs at my jokes. It's just an illusion when they say they do. I know better.

Now you may wish to conclude that I am practicing paranoia or that I am going a bit nutty, and that it's not regression to my childhood at all. You may think I'm odd or enjoying a bit of dementia.

Well, scoff if you will. You don't even exist as far as I'm concerned. Out of my orbit, you're a nothing. You do not exist. There are no pigeons on the roof. My wife is an illusion. The multi-colored papers in our mailboxes flip in and out by themselves to announce non-events. All is nothing at all, except me.

Hee, hee, hee.

I'm so sad, so very sad

Through many years, oh quite a few,
I'd leave my collar quite askew.
Knew I could count, as sure as light,
Some nurturing lass would set it right.

Today a guarded veil denies
A friendly glint from women's eyes.
The burdens of distrust and fear
Have quenched the spark of yesteryear.

A broad disquiet frights lone lady,
Who now includes me with the shady.
I mourn her need of stepped-up tread
And miss the spice on which I fed.

Now my collar stands each day on end,
No female fuss nor hand to lend.
I still have hope on every trip,
But daily now, my score is zip.

I'm so sad...yes, yes...so sad.

Swimmin' with bowlegged women

When I was in college over 65 years ago, a friend sang this little ditty:

"I love to go swimmin' with bowlegged women and dive between their legs." That's all he remembered of the song, and he promised to get the rest of it, but he never did.

The words stayed with me over the years, and I have from time to time tried vainly to locate the source of the couplet. I searched the Internet for possible origins and discovered the couplet was sung by Popeye the Sailor Man. I have finally decided I can no longer let the ditty haunt me. Here is my version of the entire song, which may never have existed:

I love to go swimmin'
With bowlegged women
And dive between their legs.

The sight is so stunning
And nothing as funning
As a race between their legs.

The passage is speedy
Thru fleshy and weedy
And quite respectable legs.

There's fun in the sun,
There's glee in the sea
And beer in wooden kegs.

There's joy in a toy
And a freckled-faced boy
And a dish of scrambled eggs.

There's pie in the sky
And a steal of a buy
And in drinking down to the dregs.

But best to go swimmin'
With bowlegged women
And dive between their legs.

That's best of all!

Gulled in the Florida Keys

In December 1933, five Antioch College freshmen, including me, and a physical education professor traveled by station wagon from frigid Ohio to Florida on a Christmas break. In a few days, we had successfully trolled for oysters, harvested oranges, seen sponges unloaded, visited an exotic fruit farm, and basked in the hot sun.

Pleased with our Florida trip thus far, we turned south and eagerly headed for the Florida Keys. As we tanked up in a Key Largo Esso station, we noisily admired the rare and brilliant seashells on display there. Skinny, the attendant, suggested it would be easy to get such a collection of our own if we wanted one. "You won't have no trouble. When you get to the town of Perky, ask for Jerry in the fishing shack and tell him Skinny sent you. He'll gladly show you where to find them."

Visions of abalone danced in our heads. We didn't know a cowry from a cockle shell, a scallop from a lightning whelk, but Skinny had whetted our appetites for some of these glittery beauties. What wonderful Christmas gifts we would be taking home!

As predicted, Jerry turned out to be "real friendly" and eager to please. "Them's the keys over there where the shells are plentiful," he assured us. "And that one where the birds are feeding is the best of all."

A channel of several hundred feet separated us from the treasures. "How do we get there?" we asked.

"Nothing to it. You just wade over. Water's no deeper than your knees. Here's some old gunny sacks you can borrow, and good luck."

We removed our shoes and socks, rolled up our trousers, and slinging the sacks over our shoulders, we stepped into the water.

"Wait just a minute," Jerry shouted. "I think I should mention one little problem you could have. Sometimes a kind of double-jawed stingray swims in the channel, and they can be dangerous unless you take proper care."

That stopped us dead in our barefoot tracks.

He went on, "I didn't mean to scare you fellows, but

the rays ain't no real problem so long as you move a stick around and beat the top of the water. That scares hell out of them. Those tree branches piled over there are used all the time by seashell pickers, and no one's been bit for seven years."

Reassured, we each picked up a branch and proceeded across the waterway, beating the surface as we moved. Jerry's estimate of the depth was more than slightly skewed, because as we advanced to our destination, the water became deeper.

It crept over our ankles to our knees, over our knees to our thighs, up over our trousers to our hips, over our hips to our chests, where it lingered, making it extremely difficult to keep beating the water with the branches.

Our progress was slow, but finally to our relief the water shallowed, and we began to emerge. We had gotten wet and were a bit breathless, but it did not matter now that we had reached our objective.

Mollusks do indeed like the gently shelving sandy and muddy shores of warm southern waters, but in the mysterious ways of the tropics, word of our predatory intentions must have reached the whole seashell community, for not a single shell was anywhere in sight. The key was bald—barren of everything except a host of laughing gulls that greeted us raucously as we approached. But theirs was not the only sound we heard.

Back on the causeway, where only Jerry had stood alone when we departed, the road now overflowed with cars and scores of the townspeople of Perky—men, women and children. Their collective shouts and laughter rolled out to us loud and clear.

We five collegians and the professor from the frozen north, armed with branches for frantically beating off the stingrays in the "deep" water on the way to the barren key, had been thoroughly gulled!

And I can't even milk a cow!

I am just a big-city boy. I grew up in the vicinity of New York City, but always in northern New Jersey. As long as I knew them, my parents always had candy stores. In one of my earliest memories, I swiped a chocolate bar, but unlike the Greek goddess Aphrodite who threw down the Golden Apple and got away, I threw down the chocolate bar but was caught.

What has that got to do with milking a cow? Well, nothing really, but it is a good story, and I wanted you to know that you cannot rely on Greek mythology if you want to get away with anything important. In those days I was called Herschel by my mother and father. My school records, however, always listed me as Harry.

Many years later, as a young adult, I needed my birth certificate. I wrote to the Department of Vital Statistics in Newark and applied for a copy in my name of Harry Weiss. I had been born in the German Hospital (renamed the Memorial Hospital during World War I) on July 15, 1915. There was no Harry in the books, but there was a Herman born to my parents on that date. It is fair to assume that was me.

Whatever the procedures were, I followed them and restored my good name to the record books as Harry. Years have passed since, one piled up on another.

My daughter, who is doing genealogical research on the family, has gone back to early census records and has discovered that the census taker had referred in one census to my two brothers correctly as Carl and William but to me as Hyman!

So now, late in life, I have learned that I have been known as Herschel, Harry, Herman and Hyman. They are four "H's" and of course, that makes me eligible for membership in the Four-H Club. That is an honor I must refuse. It is an agriculture youth group, and I DON'T EVEN KNOW HOW TO MILK A COW!

My fling with LBJ

As the Commerce Department press officer, I was invited one day to the White House with several other Department officials to watch President Lyndon B. Johnson sign legislation important to our department. It was a routine event at which we assembled in the Green Room and heard the President describe the importance of the new law.

At the ceremony's end, we were all lined up and told to exit along a corridor down the north side of the building and out the main entrance. Our names were announced, and moments later we were shaking the hand of the President.

His was a firm handshake. He looked you in the eye and said, "Glad you could come." Then he smiled, and at that instant, a blinding flash told you your picture had been taken with LBJ.

A few days later, an 8x10-inch print of the encounter was in my hand. I knew the photo was not too meaningful; I had no real relationship with the president, but I had a copy made and sent it to my parents.

A few weeks later, I was invited to the White House again for a similar event. When it was over, we were lined up as before for the picture taking. As I neared the President I raised my hand in a friendly "hi" and walked by. I already had my picture. I did not need another one, but Lyndon Johnson did not know that.

I had hardly gone two strides beyond when he reached out his long arm, grabbed my hand and yanked. Talk about the power of the Presidency—I suddenly found myself hoisted through the air, and in mid-flight, the photo-light flashed.

I tried to mumble an explanation for my disregard of the niceties, but he pushed me along toward the exit. I waited for a picture showing me in midair being yanked by the most powerful arm of the most powerful government on earth, but it never came.

The effect on my parents of the picture I had sent them was electric. They came from poor Jewish families in a small village in Austria-Hungary—now a part of Poland.

Figure 7. Harry Weiss meets President Lyndon B. Johnson.

What a bombshell seeing their baby son shaking hands with the President! It was as if they themselves had been invited to dine with Franz Joseph, Emperor of Austria and King of Hungary. Every relative received copies, and every neighbor in their small New Jersey town saw the picture. By return mail, my mother wrote the following letter:

Dear Harry:

We got the Picture of you and the President of the Unitet States of America and I am very glad to be alife on tis moment to see one of our sons potograft with the President of America its great and we are very Happy and we wish the President of a long life and a Happi life and we will vote for him again and I am sure he will be again President for another 4 years. With love from Mom-Pop and we are very prout of you. I will have it framt when you will visit us.

I have never before nor since had so much pleasure from a photograph. I also had it "framt," with my mother's letter largely obscuring Lyndon Johnson's features.

Part Three.
April Fool Stories

Revolutionary conveyor-belt medicine planned for MPP

A revolutionary, one-stop medical examination process—a system of specially designed gurneys transporting patients on conveyor belts—is being considered for Maplewood Park Place by a subcommittee of the Advisory Health Services Committee.

The installation, estimated to cost $750,000, would require structural changes in Maplewood: breaking through the wall of the current East Wing clinic and laying down multi-layered, high-grade conveyor belt tracks along one side of the clubroom, out to the patio, across the patio, and back along the other side of the clubroom, past the arts room to the corridor.

Invented by the Hold-the-Mayo Step-Brothers of Deltoid, Nebraska, the device is known as the Conveyor Belt Automatic Health Android Complex (CONBAYHAC).

"This is a one-shot medical examination in which a thirty-minute transit through the system will provide a thorough and completely reliable evaluation of everything that ails you, could ail you and may never ail you," said a knowledgeable resident on the committee who had seen CONBAYHAC in action.

It will be optional for all MPP residents who may wish to simplify their medical relationships with their many different doctors. The machine will readily take the place of their cardiologists, internists, neurologists, cardio-vascular surgeons, proctologists, urologists, acupuncturists, herbalists, podiatrists, manicurists and others. Many HMOs are eager to invest in the device, and Medicare is considering covering the costs for the elderly.

The whole procedure will be simple enough, according to information obtained by this writer, and will require the presence of only two professionals—a nurse at the beginning and an all-purpose doctor at the end. Here's how it will work:

- A nurse will help you disrobe and slip into a paper gown in a choice of three colors—mauve, turquoise or magenta—securely tied in the back with three stout ribbons (not the flimsy two now in use in hospitals). Your clothes will be placed in a ditty bag.

- You will be asked to lie down in the specially shaped and equipped gurney and securely fastened to its snug configurations. At this point the nurse will give you an opportunity to swallow a "happy pill" to lessen any anxieties you may have about the "perfectly safe" procedure.

- Without you realizing it, preliminary probes will automatically take samples of dandruff flakes, eyelid crusts, earwax, umbilical lint and facial zits. The information will be entered into a computer.

- With a musical "toot-toot," the conveyor belt then starts its transit through the system. Along the way, probes will painlessly remove body fluids and analyze them en route. One short stop will enable you to read eye charts overhead. Another will test hearing by emitting sounds at various levels, which you must acknowledge by fluttering your eyelids.

- En route, sonic gauges will measure bone density, dental caries, cholesterol levels, arthritic compression, mental acuity, suppressed negative thoughts, and body-fat-to-height ratios.

- At one brief moment, a minor electrical shock will be applied to the right big toe, and a measurement made to record the time it takes to travel to the medulla oblongata—a significant measure of Alzheimer's Disease susceptibility.

While an effort will be made to protect patients from rain and snow showers while in transit on the uncovered patio, the inventors feel that body reactions to inclement weather will provide an additional diagnostic tool. It is known as shudder-freeze syndrome response.

"The transit will of course be halted during lightning and thunder displays," an official document declares. "We have no need to ascertain reaction to severe lightning burns, as was experienced in experiments in the Delta, Nebraska, proving grounds. One patient there received third-degree burns due to meteorological miscalculations but was merely shook up a bit."

By the time the gurney journey is completed, the attending physician will have a complete, computer-generated diagnosis already printed out for consideration by Maplewood's medical director.

Because of space considerations, residents will have

to return to their rooms in their securely tied paper gowns with their ditty bags slung over their shoulders (although the private dining room may be converted to a dressing room at a later date). Matching paper slippers may be provided. No nosy photographers will be permitted to lurk in the corridors.

It is expected Maplewood management would share the cost of the installation, to consider its adaptability to all its senior service organizations across the land.

Additional questions about the Conveyor Belt system will be answered at the Concierge Desk but GURNEY-JOURNEY pamphlets will not be made available because, of course, this is an April Fool's Day essay.

New hallway rail system planned for Maplewood!

For the ease and comfort of MPP residents and to facilitate movement within the halls of Maplewood, a miniature rail system will be installed on all floors in both the East and West Wings.

The new construction by the Engineering Department will begin after financial details are finalized by the Board of Directors, who wholeheartedly support such a system. The construction could begin as early as April 15.

As now conceived, industrial-strength, four-ply aluminum rails will be laid down the centers and full lengths of every corridor. The rails will terminate at the elevators, and two-seated electric cars (known as "Snug-Bugs") will regularly traverse the system, completing the circuits every two minutes. Guests of residents will have to wait for the return of the cars.

A resident will merely have to step out of his dwelling. The cars will automatically arrive and wait for the passenger to board and be whisked to the elevators. Electronic sensors on each car will know when to stop and start for pickup and delivery of passengers.

On the ground floor, the cars will deliver riders to the front door after a stop at the restaurant.

"The system is foolproof and safe," according to the MPP director, who will overlook its installation. "It is based on the millions of rail miles traveled in similar cars in theme parks around the country. The records show that only one tourist has been mangled in every 100,000 miles, so we will have many happy trips before we lose one of our residents."

"Residents in every section of MPP will have much to say about the installations," the director continued. "They will choose from among 23 colors for the cars; they will determine the type of padding in the seats, fluffy or hard; and best of all, they can pick the kind of warning-sound devices on each car—bells, whistles, ratchets, or horns—to warn unwary walkers."

"In corridors where dogs are kept, the cars will have dog-catchers to avoid injury to the little creatures," he added. "We have tried our level best to think of everything."

Rails will be laid in one corridor each day. On those days, residents will be bused to a nearby hotel and housed and fed overnight. Through the good offices of

MPP management, the hotel has agreed to charge only $67.65 a day. Residents will pay for the lodging, but MPP will pick up the meal charges, if under $20 a day.

Speeding up the movement of residents will guarantee greater efficiency in the many MPP programs offered here. Meetings will start on time, buses will depart on schedule, and residents will be more rested and eager to participate in more activities, it is believed.

"Best of all, our community will retain its reputation for innovation and imaginative and creative thinking on behalf of elder citizens everywhere," the director added.

Church schools to rent ballroom; swimming pool to get delinquents

To stop the effects of creeping inflation on the pocketbooks of residents, Maplewood Park Place authorities are signing a series of contracts with local religious schools and the Montgomery County prison system to boost MPP annual income by $300,000.

The plan will provide class space for kindergarten children who are being turned away at crowded neighboring church schools, synagogues, and mosques. Here is the plan as outlined by a member of the Sources of New Income Committee (SNICOM) of the Board of Directors:

- The ballroom will be converted into three separate rooms for Catholic, Jewish, and Muslim children. Suggested originally by St. Jane's Catholic Church, the plan was accepted only if the other religions were included.

- To provide space for continuing MPP programs, an off-the-shelf modular ballroom unit will be purchased from The Portafab Building Co. in Chesterfield, Maryland, for $100,000. The elements will be brought in on trucks and assembled on the neighboring church grounds. A helicopter will then lift and place the module onto the patio outside the clubroom. The new room will include Bionnaire Galileo, digital-power spaceheaters and coolers. Designed for dancing Latin dances, the floor will be of toe-tested wood of the Argentinean baobab tree. The walls will be of weatherproof commercial-grade-AAA molybdenum siding built to resist 45-mile-per-hour winds. (Higher winds are rare in this area.) A Wurlitzer Nickelodeon will provide the entertainment.

- The Chevy Chase, the Bethesda, and the Annapolis rooms will be renamed the Sharon, the Theresa, and Bin-Laden rooms (STABS for short), to accommodate the three religious faiths. Jewish and Muslim children will be on each end, separated by Catholics. The piano lounge will feature events to encourage the children to love each other—ice cream fetes, volleyball, three-legged races, sparring contests, and tugs of war through carted-in mud troughs. A tarp is being ordered for the piano.

- A two-sided, hers-and-his, passion-pink-painted

PortAJohns with small Rubbermaid seats will be placed in the lobby to take care of the children's needs.

- The swimming pool is being rented by prison officials at the Montgomery County Children's Detention Center in Boyds, Maryland, on Tuesdays for delinquent boys and Thursdays for the girls. The pool activities will be rewards for good behavior. West Wing elevators will be shut down on Tuesdays and Thursdays, and residents will be advised to keep their rooms locked to avoid hooliganism. Residents will be assured that delinquents will not be allowed willy-nilly to wander about the premises. MPP management will weigh in heavily against recalcitrance.

- The religious organizations will handle all the enrollments. To prevent charges of nepotism, great-grandchildren of residents will not be allowed in the kindergartens. An exception may be made for residents with delinquent great-grandchildren.

Discussions have been going on for several months between the two Maplewood Boards, and both operating boards, with no exceptions, thought the rental idea was a superb way to cure inching-up costs.

One nameless board member, however, objected vigorously to the move, "Why do we want a bunch of simpering, snot-nosed kids running about our halls and spreading their germs? The idea of a group of singing, happy kids staining our rugs, getting Tootsie Rolls stuck to the curtains, putting bubble gum on the seats and tracking mud along the corridors is unconscionable. Whose [deleted] stupid idea was it?"

This member was ejected from the deliberations for failure to appreciate the worthiness of new ideas and was shunned by the group. It was said he is moving.

The vote was then unanimous by both committees. The various purchase arrangements, leases, binding agreements and delivery schedules are to be signed at a closed meeting in the sales office on April Fool's Day. Residents seeking clarification will meet with the sales office after the signing sessions at 5 p.m.

Food production center to replace Maplewood swimming pool

Responding to unsettling conditions of war with Iraq, lagging nation-building in Afghanistan, nuclear threats from North Korea, and the possibility of runaway inflation caused by recent economic moves, a decision has been reached to convert the Maplewood swimming pool to a food-growing center.

Arguments have been raging for weeks between two intensely divided sections of a committee appointed by the Board of Directors to seek budgetary reduction. Suggestions included the pool-closing possibility. Until now, the arguments have been kept quiet because of the unsettling conditions in the country, but the final decision now appears certain.

Three-quarters of the committee fought vehemently

and appear to have won the battle for converting the pool to a *hydroponics food-producing unit,* anticipating continuous food shortages caused by possible terrorist attacks throughout the country that would disturb food-distribution facilities.

A member of this group used this argument: "We have to recognize that we must economize, that our costs will skyrocket. Those who miss the pool can just hop gaily around and splash water in their bathtubs and otherwise get their exercise on the marvelous new equipment in the workout room. The money we save for lifeguards, heated pool, towels and pool maintenance far surpasses the expenses for our suggested change."

"Hydroponics is the answer. We have the space. The pool is an ideal size to provide our community with food-stuffs during our national crisis. For a few bucks—maybe $2,500 for pumps, lamps, nutrients, temperature-control equipment, roots and seeds—we can have a never-ending supply of foods that will disappear from our markets. Not only do hydroponics foods grow more quickly and abundantly in an aqueous environment, but we can grow exotic foods we have not enjoyed before."

His eyes glittered as he listed such foods as South African giant legumes, Chilean purple peppers, Guatemalan Chichi fruits and famous equatorial flammerjams. "A hydroponics food center is a real necessity in these perilous times," he concluded.

The other members, headed by a former military notable, reported his group had opted for a tennis-badminton court in place of the expensive swimming pool.

"The war will be over in a breeze, no fuss, no muss, but we will have to economize as a result of the conflict and rebuilding of Iraq," he asserted. "We must close the pool and reduce expenses."

"Except for an inexpensive but sturdy floor cover construction of an outdoor-type No. 207 AstroTurf atop No. 2 Oregon hardwood multi-layered construction, we'd have a tennis court in a hurry. And more of our residents will get exercise and have fun. The users can buy the birds and balls themselves."

The colonel visualized contests between the East and West Wings and much hilarity among the contestants. Prizes would be given for agility, form and earnestness. "A tennis-badminton court makes sense. The war will be over in a jiffy, and we need not worry about food supplies," he said flatly.

Another resident suggested it would be more prudent to cover the empty pool with duct tape and plastic sheets to create a shelter against chemical and biological warfare, but he was ignored by the committee.

He complained vehemently. "I don't know why I was not listened to. The Director of Homeland Security has said we should create a secure place where we can gather for a few days, and the covered pool would be perfect. Duct tape is cheap. Who wants to bat balls and birds around as we are being threatened by al Qaeda villains? Is there no common sense in this place?"

The committee is to meet April Fool's Day for a final decision on the pool closure. It may not be too late for you to be heard.

Maplewood plans soccer field to replace main lobby

Responding to requests from a select group of Maplewood Park Place residents to sponsor a competitive soccer league for grandchildren in this and other retirement communities, MPP's manager today announced a series of sweeping moves to make it possible.

The playing field will be located in an extended main entrance in the building, he said. Here's the plan for the changes:

- Starting immediately, all the easy chairs, lamps, tables, plantings and mirrors will be removed from the main lobby entrance area and placed in the Flea Market for immediate sale to benefit loyal employees.

- The elaborate carpeting will be torn up and given to rug dealers for bankruptcy sales, with proceeds to help feed Iraqi children.

- Durable green AstroTurf will immediately replace the rugs. (We got a great deal from the old Cleveland Browns football franchise, according to MPP's manager.)

- Pansy beds outside the front entrance will be dug up and replaced with poison ivy and oak. Picnic benches will be placed there as a convenience for visiting teams. (It's just good strategy, says MPP's manager. "The little buggers will be so busy scratching themselves we'll just whip their behinds! We do want MPP teams to be the best in the whole retirement community system," he added.)

- Walls to the executive offices will be torn down and bleachers erected for grandparents of participants. New offices will be erected on Level G-2 from which favored residents will be assigned "visitors" places outside on the Old Georgetown Road side.
- TV cameras will be strategically placed so that residents without competing grandchildren will be able to follow the action on their home video sets on Channel 94.
- The concierge desk will be placed between the doors at the entrance so that the credentials of all players may be checked against lists provided by the residents. (We have to guard against grandchildren in their 30s and 40s being smuggled in as ringers, according to MPP's manager.)
- Special gourmet chili dogs will be the only menu on soccer days, but transportation will be provided residents to restaurants of their choice within a ten-mile radius. MPP will cover the cost of those meals up to $9.95 each, according to MPP's manager. He urged residents to try the chili dogs. "We will be serving Hebrew National Kosher franks," he said, "and everyone knows these are foods of distinction."
- All MPP dogs and cats will be specially-trained to sniff out possible marijuana users among visiting teams.
- Areas will be cleared in the assisted living area to provide quarters for two new families. One retired couple will be former Cockneys renowned for pro-

ducing rowdy spectators; the other an imported pair from Venezuela, grandparents of world-renowned soccer players.

- And LOTS more!

MPP's manager said the soccer decision was just the beginning of efforts to make life happier at MPP. "We will gladly consider any other reasonable changes to our current policies. One cannot rest on one's laurels. It's ever onward, and upward, and forward to make Maplewood Park Place the most progressive retirement community in the entire world."

Electric scooter rink planned for rear of Maplewood Park Place

A $2-million-dollar scooter rink and park may be built in the two acres of land between Maplewood Park Place and the neighboring townhouses, according to a proposal of a special steering committee.

Responding to demands of a handful of electric scooter users here for more meaningful and vigorous recreational activities, the multifaceted plan calls for:

- Construction of a covered pavilion with a multi-linear Venezuelan hardwood raceway for scooter speed competitions.
- A T-bar, Aspen-grade ski lift to carry scooters down the 20-foot drop from the road to the racetrack level and back.

- Picnic benches and hot dog dispensing machines for spectators.
- A 25-foot concrete-and-Carrara-crushed-marble sound barrier wall between the pavilion and townhouses.
- A parking area to the right of the MPP front entrance, where the flower beds are now located, large enough to accommodate 25 scooters, with a multi-purpose 12-volt battery charger included.
- A fenced-off, scooter-friendly, narrow lane of imported red brick construction from the main entrance to the T-bar lift.
- Bargain-priced, state-of-the-art scooters sold by Scooters for Seniors Ltd. Size and power of the scooters will be related to square footage of apartments owned by the residents.
- Employment of a full time Scooter-Rooter—a publicity director to promote sales of vacant MPP residences based on the pavilion novelty.
- GEICO-guaranteed insurance policies with significant discounts for those obtaining Scooters for Seniors safe-driver certificates.
- Periodic competitions with contestants from senior service communities all over America and later as a new sport in the next quadrennial Olympics in Greece.

Asked about the project, a member of the scooter booster committee said, "I have had my sweet, three-wheel chartreuse scooter for five years, and it's back and forth, forth and back to the dining room and the circle out front. We scooterers need some excitement, and the pavilion will provide it. Since many others here will ultimately need scooters, it's a wonderful opportunity for easy purchase now at discount prices and training in their use."

Each resident would be required to contribute a proportionate share of the initial $2,000,000 investment. Ongoing costs will be covered by large businesses in exchange for corporate logos on the pavilion walls and on tee shirts worn by scooter drivers. Discussions are under way with One-a-Day Vitamins, Rubbermaid Heating Pads, Phillips Milk of Magnesia, Nike, and Estee Lauder. The Pepsi-Cola for Health Pavilion name is already in negotiation.

Questioned why these plans have not been discussed at public meetings where so many ideas are explored, MPP's manager declined comment and claimed executive privilege. It was learned, however, that he supported this development for its potential use throughout the entire corporate retirement community system. Premature disclosure might have wrecked the plans, it was alleged.

MPP's manager has promised to answer questions and solicit approval of residents at a meeting in the Ball Room from 2 to 4 p.m. on April Fool's Day.

Part Four.

What Those Nursery Rhymes Really Mean

Three blind mice, revisited

Three blind mice. See how they run.
They all run after the farmer's wife,
Who cut off their tails with a carving knife.
Did you ever see such a sight in your life
As three blind mice?

Pardon me, but I do not believe that story! I have given it much thought, and I believe it was the farmer's wife who was blind, and the three *fine* mice had excellent vision. Here is how the action really took place:

One day, three *fine* mice were hungry, and the farmer's wife was baking her favorite multigrain-and-raisin bread. Her instructions were in Braille and included two tablespoons of honey, preferably Clover Grade AA. That is why it was so delicious!

One fine mouse said to another, "Let us pretend we're passing strangers. We are starving and need a handout." They crawled up a table leg and reached the tabletop as she was removing the loaf from the oven, and they plaintively cried that they were three starving travelers and would appreciate a slice of her world-renowned bread.

Well, of course, the kind-hearted farmer's wife, a Florence Nightingale at heart, was glad to help the hungry travelers. As she started to slice the loaf with her four-loaf cleaver, the mice heard a noise in the front of the farmhouse and were afraid it was the farmer, who could see very well. They turned to check, and just then the knife descended, and their tails were cut off along with the slice of bread...one, two, three, four. You never saw such a sight in your life as three tail-less fine mice.

Now I have envisioned a more realistic scenario. Those three mice were *blonde* mice—or albinos. A widespread belief exists to this day that albinos are agents of the devil. They tell long, scary, dishonest *tales* that have to be cut off or contradicted as soon as possible to avoid havoc in the community. My poem goes:

Three blonde mice. See how they lie.
Their tales must be cut by maligned and mad wives,
Who suffer disgrace from the degrading lies.
Did you ever in your life hear such terrible tales,
As from three blonde mice?"

As I was a little frustrated over which story to go with, I have looked it up on the Internet. There I found that that the farmer's wife really referred to Queen Mary I, the daughter of King Henry VIII. She was a staunch Catholic, and the three blind mice referred to three noblemen who, to her intense annoyance, adhered blindly to the Protestant faith. They were burnt at the stake. She was known as the farmer's wife because of the massive estates that she and her husband possessed.

Naaah! You don't believe that story, do you?

The real skinny on Miss Muffet

Little Miss Muffet
Sat on her tuffet
Eating her curds and whey.
Along came a spider
Who sat down beside her
And frightened Miss Muffet away.

Something is wrong with that tale. It has all kinds of hidden meanings, and I think I have broken the code. For one thing, to "muff it" is to miss the big opportunity—you go for something, and it fails to happen. The tuffet must also be a hidden code for toughing it out. Sitting on a tuffet indeed! She was a wayward child who roughed it. The rough get tough, when the going gets rough.

Now we get to the heart of the matter: What she was doing when some guardian of the law—perhaps a narc disguised as a Spiderman—sat next to her? The rhyme says "curds and whey"—but she was checking some stuff in a "hurried way."

I think she was testing and was wary of the quality of new marijuana in her possession. She was testing to see if it was real Colombian or just some weed that had been foisted on her. She picked up her bag and raced away, leaving the narc behind, drove through dark alleys, raced through abandoned hovels, and finally reached the group house she shared with a number of homeless but enterprising drop-outs.

What supported the motley group was a profitable cookie business among the affluent suburban wives who were enjoying wild weekend parties by eating marijuana-laced oatmeal cookies. By word of mouth, the availability of the cookies had spread through Westchester.

Little Miss Muffet, as the prime cook, supervised the baking of the mood-raising confection, whose batter required much intense stirring to be sure that the drug was evenly divided through the whole batch.

Wouldn't you know that one day Miss Muffet was a bit high from an overdose of the drug, and the baking of cookies fell to careless Dick Witless. He failed to stir the dough thoroughly, and the Colombian stash all settled in just one cookie.

By a damnable coincidence, that cookie was eaten by the wife of the police chief. She went berserk from ingesting the concentrated marijuana cookie. She screamed and gnashed her teeth, and raced around ripping at her clothes and pulling her hair. She hollered at her husband, calling him a no-good official who couldn't keep laced cookies off the streets.

Someone called the poison control bureau anonymously and was told to dunk her in an ice-cold bath for 20 minutes, dry her off well, and take her for a long walk in the frigid weather. She did not die, her cholesterol stayed low, but that was the end of the joy-inducing cookies.

The group homes with all the delinquents were raided and shut down by the police chief, effectively ending the weekend parties. The suburban women then turned to such games as Canasta, Mah-jongg, and Keno. The more daring went to the clubhouse and played novel games with the staff while their husbands played golf.

That is the real story of Miss Muffet.

Then I explored the Internet to see if any historical precedent existed for the rhyme we were taught. Here's what I found:

Miss Muffet was allegedly a 16th Century little girl whose name was Patience. Her father, Dr. Thomas Muffet (possibly Moffett or Moufet), an entomologist who died in 1604, wrote *The Silkwormes and their Flies*, a "lively yarn described in verse." Patience did not share her father's love of bugs. One morning while eating breakfast, one of her father's bugs appeared. She leapt up, spilling the curds and whey, and ran out of the house.

The first extant version is dated 1805 in *Songs for the Nursery*, whose 1812 edition read "Little Mary Ester sat upon a tester..." Halliwell's 1842 collection read "Little Miss Mopsey sat in a shopsey..."

You don't believe any of these explanations, do you?

The true story of Jack and Jill

Jack and Jill went up the hill
To fetch a pail of water.
Jack fell down and broke his crown
And Jill came tumbling after.

That is the rhyme we were taught, and I don't believe it for one moment. For one thing, Jill's father was a dowser, who used a hickory stick to find underground water supplies. He had never found water on the hill, despite his success in other locations. He believed Jack and Jill were up to some hanky-panky, and the pail was just a diversion. He followed them up the hill one day.

I hate to report that Jack and Jill were in *flagrante delicto* when he peered behind the old oak tree there. With the switch he broke Jack's crown and sent him tumbling down the hill. He grabbed Jill by the ear and escorted her home amid accusations and disgust for such behavior.

Now that would be the end of it, but for the fact that after a few months, Jill showed unmistakable signs of pregnancy. Who could have fathered that child except Jack or the young barber for whom Jack worked as a shoeshine boy? The barber had also dated her a few times.

These were days before DNA testing, but the dowser wracked his brain, and he thought that if he put the hickory switch secretly into the bed with Jill, it would somehow divine who was the father when swung over the heads of the young men.

Retrieving the switch the next day, he entered the barbershop where the proprietor was shaving the mayor whose shoes were being shined by Jack. As was his wont, he circled the chair with the divining rod, and the switch plunged down AND STRUCK THE MAYOR!

He apologized profusely and fled the scene. What else could he do to establish the parenthood? Then he had a Solomon-like idea. One day, when his by-now-well-rounded daughter was resting by the Watahoochie stream, he decided to push her into the water, knowing full well she was a good swimmer.

He ran to the barbershop and yelled, "Help, help! My daughter has fallen into the Watahoochie, and we must run to her aid!" He knew full well from reading the Bible that against all odds, a real father would dive in to save his unborn child.

Jack, the barber, and the mayor raced to the Watahoochie, but it was the mayor who dived in to try to save Jill. (He later claimed it was just civic duty.) Meanwhile, as she was floating unfazed downstream, a young fellow named Floyd Williams, who was fishing at the bridge, saw Jill and hauled her in with his hook and line.

Some months before, Floyd and Jill had attended the Watahoochie Barn Frolics. They had become so deliriously carried away by the do-si-do-ing and the fermented apple cider that afterwards they had retreated to the back of the barn and had enjoyed a little unprotected intimacy. Well, the long and short of it is, that when Floyd saw her condition and calculated the time lapse, he stepped up as a gentleman and proposed, and they were married. Remember, this was in the good old days.

Just to see if historians were putting their own spin on the story, I looked up incident on the Internet.

One historian says that this rhyme was about two powerful religious leaders who served under King Henry VIII of England. It says, "In 1518, the two leaders—a cardinal and a bishop—tried to settle a feud between France and Rome. They failed, and a war broke out. The cardinal sent British troops to fight against France and raised taxes—not lowered them—to pay for the war." The people of England hated the two leaders, and it is said that this rhyme was invented to make fun of them.

Now I ask you: Which story makes more sense, mine or theirs?

The modern story of Humpty Dumpty

Humpty Dumpty sat on a wall.
Humpty Dumpty had a great fall.
All the King's horses and all the King's men
Couldn't put Humpty together again.

In an almost unbelievable way, that nursery rhyme parallels a story of our times. It really is a sad tale of Humphrey Dumster, the famous Universal King Pictures star and his great fall from the public's grace. He was riding high, with one successful blockbuster B movie after another.

His photo sat on every wall advertising his current movies. You will remember such exciting films as "How Mars Was Turned Into a Candy Bar," "The Elusive Werewolves of Utica Falls," "Three Cohens in a Fountain," and "Foxy and the Strange Tail." They were all running in New York at the same time. He was having a great autumn, his greatest fall of any year.

One day as he left his penthouse suite at the Commodore in New York, he remembered he had to make an important phone call. As he had no coins in his pocket to do so, and he was passing a Salvation Army bell-ringer at the time, so in all innocence he dropped a five-dollar bill into the kettle and reached in for a quarter and a dime so he could make his missed call. What a mistake that was!

This innocent exchange of currency happened in front of a bank building whose camera clicked just as Humphrey was retrieving the coins. Next morning the *New York Daily News* and the *Daily Mirror* ran the picture, leaked to the paparazzi, of Humphrey as his hands reached into the kettle, and its headlines read MOVIE STAR CAUGHT ROBBING BLIND MAN! and MILLIONAIRE STAR HOOKED BY CROOK! The photo soon circulated around the world.

TV shouters repeated the story over and over, pointing out how the rich were robbing the poor. The blind man himself appeared on TV and answered such profound questions as, "Describe your feelings when you learned you were robbed by a famous star."

Humphrey tried in vain to prove that he had dropped a five-dollar bill in the kettle, but there were many fives in there at the time (this was near the Commodore, after all), and no one thought to check for fingerprints or DNA.

Because of the widespread publicity, a divorced wife was able to serve him with a subpoena in which he was charged with wife-abuse, deliquent child-support payments and child abandonment. This even made the front page of *The New York Times*.

Is not this a sad story of how in a hapless moment one's life can be turned into a mess? He had been a star for a decade for King's Universal, and all the King's officers and their publicity men flooded the newspapers and TV news outlets trying to put Humphrey's reputation together again. It was futile, and Humphrey fell completely apart.

I will not dwell on Humphrey's demise or sermonize on how, ironically, he turned to the Salvation Army and became a bell-ringer himself. But it I cannot tell a lie, for he is now a beachcomber in the Bahamas somewhere. The original, blind bell-ringer is now a commentator on *Fox News*.

Now, what do the historians say about the old nursery rhyme? Humpty Dumpty was a common nickname for people of large proportions in the 1400s. This rhyme refers to King Richard III of England. The Battle of Bosworth took place on August 22, 1485. It was the fight for the throne between King Richard III and the head of the house of Lancaster, Henry Tudor. Richard sat on his horse atop Ambion Hill ready for battle, directing his armies, when he was murdered.

Other suggested origins are that during the English Civil War (1642-49), "Humpty Dumpty" was the name for powerful cannon. It was mounted atop the St. Mary's Wall Church in Colchester to defend the city against siege in the summer of 1648. (Colchester was a Parliamentarian stronghold, but it had been captured by Royalists, and they held it for 11 weeks.) The enemy hit the church tower and the top was blown off. "Humpty Dumpty" fell off and tumbled to the ground. The King's men tried to fix him but to no avail.

Follow the money, Jack Horner

Little Jack Horner
Sat in the corner,
Eating a Christmas pie.
He put in his thumb,
And pulled out a plum,
And said, "What a good boy am I!"

We did not know when we were children what this nursery rhyme was all about. Well, I am happy to announce that I have broken the code and am willing to share it with you!

- He was not little, but a little person—a midget.
- Jack was not his first name. It was Cassius. Like

Jack, Cash was another name for money.

- Horner's real last name was Bugler. He was Cash Bugler, sometime known as "Moolah" Bugler.
- He worked for a traveling circus and spent his time serving as "The Smallest Man in the World," but between appearances in the sideshow, he was particularly skillful as the circus accountant and bookkeeper, hence the name Moolah.

A little research found in the *Annals of Circustry* (Feb. 14, 1823, Vol. 243) shows that all was well in The Wonders of the World Circus until it was joined by towering Tanya Muscletoff, a Bulgarian who was billed as THE WORLD'S TALLEST WOMAN. Truth to tell, she was only six-foot-two, but with two-foot stilts under her denims she appeared a giant.

Well, I do not want to keep you in suspense any longer, but strange as it may seem, Moolah fell in love with Tanya, and Tanya fell in love with the idea that Moolah held the key to her return to Plovdiv in Bulgaria, where her father and one brother worked in a plant that made rowboats for use on the Maritsa River.

As accountant, it was Moolah's job to see how much of the circus's annual budget could be allocated to a Christmas pie—a seasonal reward—which could be divided among all the performers. Well, it was the case of small-mindedness in the tall, and tall-mindedness in the short, and Moolah was induced by Tanya to make off with the entire pie, which he did with aplomb—hence the historic confusion with a plum. We could not discover what Bulgarian wiles were used, but together the couple fled to New York.

They fled in the middle of the night when all slept but the three elephants—Ike, Dick and George—who usually sounded the alarm when strange movements were detected on the circus grounds. Twelve Mister Goodbars and three hands of bananas had silenced the three pachyderms.

Tanya said, "What a good boy was Moolah," before she ran off with the loot, leaving the midget stranded at La Guardia as Tanya departed for Bulgaria. Moolah now hides in a monkey suit in Bolivia, where he works for an organ grinder. Warrants are now out for their arrest.

Here is what an old English history book tells us happened: The Bishop of Glastonbury sent his steward, Jack Horner, to King Henry VIII with a Christmas gift—a pie in which were hidden the title deeds to twelve manorial estates. On his way to the king, Jack popped open the pie and stole the deed to the Manor of Mells, a real plum of an estate. To this day the Horner family resides there.

Nah, who can go for that tale?

Quick Order Form

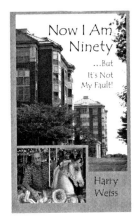

For additional copies of
Now I Am Ninety
by Harry Weiss

Order by phone: 540-987-9536
Order on the web: *www.blackwaterpublications.com*
Order by e-mail: *blackwaterpub@earthlink.net*
Order by mail: Fill out the form below (please print)

_____

NAME

_____

ADDRESS

_____

CITY, STATE, ZIP

Enclose $12.95 for each copy, plus $4 for shipping one
book, or $5 for two books. Virginia residents, add 5%
sales tax ($0.65) or $13.60 per book, plus shipping.

Make check payable to *Blackwater Publications*.

Mail this form and check to:

> Blackwater Publications
> P.O. Box 80
> Boston, VA 22713

Money-back guarantee: Returnable for full refund
if you are unsatisfied for any reason.